Promoting a Web Site on th

A practical guide to attracting visitors using online and traditional techniques

Internet Handbooks

1001 Web Sites for Writers on the Internet
Books and Publishing on the Internet
Building a Web Site on the Internet
Careers Guidance on the Internet
Chat & Chat Rooms on the Internet
Creating a Home Page on the Internet
Discussion Forums on the Internet
Education & Training on the Internet
Exploring Yahoo! on the Internet
Finding a Job on the Internet
Getting Connected to the Internet
Getting Started on the Internet
Gardens & Gardening on the Internet
Graduate Job Hunting on the Internet
Homes & Property on the Internet
Human Resource Management on the Internet
Internet Explorer on the Internet
Internet for Schools
Internet for Students
Internet for Writers
Internet Skills for the Workplace
Law & Lawyers on the Internet
Linking Your Web Site on the Internet
Marketing Your Business on the Internet
Music & Musicians on the Internet
Naming a Web Site on the Internet
News and Magazines on the Internet
Overseas Job Hunting on the Internet
Personal Finance on the Internet
Pets on the Internet
Promoting a Web Site on the Internet
Protecting Children on the Internet
Shops & Shopping on the Internet
Studying English on the Internet
Studying Law on the Internet
Travel & Holidays on the Internet
Using Credit Cards on the Internet
Using Email on the Internet
Using Netscape on the Internet
Where to Find It on the Internet
Wildlife & Conservation on the Internet
Working from Home on the Internet
Your Privacy on the Internet

Other titles in preparation

Promoting a Web Site
on the internet

A practical guide to attracting visitors using online and traditional techniques

Graham Jones
BSc (Hons)

www.internet-handbooks.co.uk

Other Internet Handbooks by the same author

Naming a Web Site on the Internet
Personal Finance on the Internet
Protecting Children on the Internet
Travel and Holidays on the Internet
Using Credit Cards on the Internet

Copyright © 2000 by Graham Jones

First published in 2000 by Internet Handbooks, a Division of International Briefings Ltd, Plymbridge House, Estover Road, Plymouth PL6 7PY, United Kingdom.

Customer services tel:	(01752) 202301
Orders fax:	(01752) 202333
Customer services email:	cservs@plymbridge.com
Distributors web site:	www.plymbridge.com
Internet Handbooks web site:	www.internet-handbooks.co.uk

All rights reserved. No part of this work may be reproduced or stored in an information retrieval system without the express permission of the Publishers given in writing.

Graham Jones has asserted his moral right to be identified as the author of this work.

Note: The contents of this book are offered for the purposes of general guidance only and no liability can be accepted for any loss or expense incurred as a result of relying in particular circumstances on statements made in this book. Readers are advised to check the current position with the appropriate authorities before entering into personal arrangements.

Case studies in this book are entirely fictional and any resemblance to real persons or organisations is entirely coincidental.

Printed and bound by The Cromwell Press Ltd, Trowbridge, Wiltshire.

Contents

List of illustrations 7

Preface 9

1 Establishing your web site's identity 11

    Establishing a brand 11
    Choosing the right domain name 16
    Making sure your web site is professional 16
    Ensuring your systems are robust 17
    Promotional follow up 18
    The secrets of successful planning 18

2 Getting listed in search engines 20

    Making your pages 'search engine friendly' 21
    Using meta tags 21
    Using meta tag analysis software 26
    Meta tags and frames 28
    Making your pages acceptable to search engines 30
    Submitting your site to search engines 31
    Submitting your site manually 31
    Using automatic submission services 31
    Using software to submit your site 32
    Using web services to submit your site 36
    Repeating your submission 37
    Reviewing the search engine submission process 38

3 Applying to the top search engines 39

    AltaVista 39
    Ask Jeeves 41
    Excite 42
    Google 43
    HotBot 43
    Infoseek 44
    LookSmart 45
    Lycos 46
    MSN 47
    ScrubTheWeb 48
    Snap 49
    Webcrawler 50
    Yahoo!

4 Getting listed throughout the web 52

    Internet directories 52
    'What's new' lists 59
    Award schemes 61
    Web rings 61
    Reciprocal links 63
    Usenet messages 64
    Increasing your hit rate 66

Contents

5	**More free online promotion**	67
	Press releases	67
	Targeted email	70
	Banner exchanges	75
	Don't fall foul of the data laws	77
	Maximising your free publicity	77
	Ensuring successful free promotion	79
6	**Paying for online promotion**	80
	Paying for search engine listings	81
	Paying for online adverts	82
	Paying for targeted email announcements	86
	Paying for online public relations activities	87
	Paying for referrals	89
	Weighing up the fee-based services	91
7	**Promotion outside the internet**	92
	Ways of promoting your web site offline	92
	Advertising contacts	93
	Direct mail contacts	94
	Public relations contacts	94
	General marketing contacts	95
	The importance of word of mouth	96
	Becoming the best	96
Table of web sites		99
Glossary of internet terms		101
Index		117

List of illustrations

Figure	Page
1. Dmitry's Design site	14
2. Clip Art UK for designs and ideas	15
3. The Web Writer service	17
4. Cyber Eye web site promotion	24
5. Webs Unlimited and MetaTag Maker	24
6. SubmitIt Corner's meta tag generator	25
7. Web Position Gold – search rankings	27
8. Submit-URL for search engines.	27
9. NetMechanic for your web site	28
10. SoftSeek submission	32
11. Submission Wizard	33
12. Page Submit Pro	34
13. Submit Wolf Pro	34
14. Traffic Builder	35
15. Online Biz submission links	36
16. Submit It from Microsoft	37
17. AltaVista, the search engine	40
18. Search Engine Watch	40
19. Ask Jeeves site submission	41
20. Excite UK site submission	42
21. Google site submission	43
22. HotBot site submission	44
23. InfoSeek site submission	45
24. LookSmart site submission	46
25. Lycos site submission	46
26. MSN site submission	47
27. Snap site submission	49
28. WebCrawler site submission	50
29. Suggest a site to Yahoo!	51
30. The 1 Dir of 1 Dirs directory	53
31. The Aleph Search directory	53
32. AllSearch Engines	54
33. Searchability reviews	55
34. Scoot UK business directory	57
35. The Open Directory Project	58
36. The UK Plus directory	59
37. Yellow Pages and free listings	60
38. Get a listing in What's Nu	60
39. Web site award schemes	61
40. The WebRing directory	62
41. Reciprocal Links	64
42. Newsgroup announcements	66
43. Press release writing tips	68

Illustrations

Figure	Page
44. PR Web press releases	70
45. UK Data Protection	71
46. Email and spamming	72
47. ListBot's mailing list service	73
48. The E-zine Factory	74
49. BX Exchange banner exchange	76
50. UK Banners	77
51. The Internet Marketing Center	78
52. Idea Marketers	79
53. Getting listed on Galaxy	80
54. GoTo.com – the search engine you pay for	82
55. bCentral Advertising Store	83
56. Ezines and email newsletters for site promotion	85
57. Postmaster Direct for targeted email	87
58. PR Newswire for press release distribution	88
59. Link Share	90
60. URL Wire	91
61. Direct Marketing Association	94
62. Public Relations Consultants Association (PRCA)	95
63. Chartered Institute of Marketing (CIM)	95

Preface

Promoting your web site is vital if it is to succeed. With more than two billion pages available on the web, your precious material will simply get lost without effective promotion. If you are running a business on the internet such promotion is essential – probably even more so than for a non-internet business. Without it, people will not know you even exist. With traditional businesses, having a physical location helps since you are at least visible to people nearby. With the internet, your customers could be anywhere in the world. They are very unlikely to 'bump into you' by accident. Hence, finding ways of promoting a web site is fundamental to the survival of an internet business, and to underestimate the task would be to dramatically diminish its chances of survival.

This book is designed to help you utilise the various powerful resources on the internet to promote your web site. Equally, it will point you towards ways in which you can promote it outside the internet – an oft-ignored but very fruitful avenue.

Unlike many other books about using the internet, this one assumes that you know the basics, and already have internet access. It assumes a certain level of technical knowledge, and that you already have the necessary equipment to log on. The book focuses on the all-important issues of the promotion you need to make a success of your web site development.

There are many web site addresses (URLs) in this book. To visit one, simply type the address, exactly as printed in this book, in the Address or Location box towards the top of the window of your web browser program. Once you have typed it in, hit the Enter key on your keyboard. You will then be transported to the web site you want.

As with any modern guidebook on a rapidly growing technology, the information is as up to date as possible at the time of going to print. If any of the sites listed have changed since I wrote about them, why not let me know, and the information can be put to use in future updates. If your company has changed its web site address, or if you want to submit details of a web site you think should be included in a future edition of this book, please email the details to:

post@grahamjones.net

Please note that, whilst every care has been taken to ensure the information contained within this book is accurate, no responsibility can be accepted for the consequences of any action taken based on the material contained within these pages. Readers should seek professional advice, which is suited to their own personal or business circumstances, before proceeding. You would also be well advised to contact computer consultants regarding any security issues.

Please also note that comments made about the web sites and other internet pages mentioned in this book are based on how they appeared at the time the book was written. Comments should not be taken as a

Preface

reflection of how a site may appear at the time you access it, unless the site has remained unchanged since this book was written.

All of the web sites shown in this book remain the copyright of their respective owners. The screen shots of web sites were correct at the time of going to press and may appear differently now. All trademarks and registered trademarks mentioned in this book are the property of their respective owners.

You will find all the links in this book at the following web site, which will be updated on a regular basis:

http://www.site-promoting.co.uk

You will also find lots of free help about the internet and ecommerce at the Internet Handbooks web site:

http://www.internet-handbooks.co.uk

Meanwhile, I hope the following pages provide you with everything you need to reap the rewards of setting up your web site in the first place.

Graham Jones

grahamjones@internet-handbooks.co.uk
http://www.grahamjones.net

1 Establishing your web site's identity

In this chapter we will explore:

- ▶ *establishing a brand*
- ▶ *choosing the right domain name*
- ▶ *making sure your web site is professional*
- ▶ *ensuring your systems are robust*
- ▶ *promotional follow up*
- ▶ *the secrets of successful planning*

Owning a web site is exciting. You can spend hours working out what you want to include, play about with the design and upload your material to the internet all on your own. The feeling that you have created something of your very own that is on display to the world is fantastic. No other technology allows you to do everything on your own, quickly and globally.

However, your sense of achievement can quickly be destroyed once you realise that you are the only viewer of your web site. The world's internet surfers will not be able to even glance at your site unless they know it is there. The real work for web sites only begins once you have finished the creative task. Promoting your web site and getting people to know it exists is the most important task you face – and it is probably the hardest.

By the middle of 2000 there were more than 20 million different web sites with billions of pages. Your web site is easily lost amongst this cacophony of noise. To try to understand how your web site can get swamped, imagine you were setting up a shop on your local high street. Even without any real promotion you would be able to sell some items. That's because your high street is probably only half a mile long and your local shoppers would be passing by.

Now picture your new shop at the end of a high street which is several thousand miles long and has shops five thousand deep. Would you get spotted now? Unlikely! Well, the web is just like this unimaginably vast high street – it's impossible to locate anything unless you know precisely where it is.

That's why successful web companies promote their businesses widely and aggressively. If they did not do this, their web sites would remain comparatively invisible. You, too, need to make significant promotional efforts if your web site is to survive.

Establishing a brand

Marketing experts everywhere have come to realise that a 'brand' is much more important in the web world than in the non-digital marketplace. True, there are some well-established brands that we buy, such as Persil or Pepsi Cola, but we also buy many unbranded goods from a host of shops and services. We simply know them or trust them, or they happen to be in the right place.

Establishing your web site's identity................................

There was an old marketing adage that there were three Ps to being successful in business – price, promotion and position. Your position was broken down into two key components – the kind of people you were aiming at, and your location. Indeed, many retail experts believe there are three Ls to success – 'location, location, location'. As you can see, the traditional wisdom doesn't really consider branding to be fundamental to success. Where you are, and the people you are aiming at, are much more important.

On the internet, it is very different:

1. Everyone is in the same location (on the viewer's computer screen).

2. Everyone can easily adapt their web site to different users to achieve a better market position.

3. Everyone can adjust their prices in an instant, because it is so easy to check the prices of the competition.

All the traditional marketing tips for success are knocked down when it comes to the internet. A new kind of marketing strategy is needed, and it has become widely accepted that a 'brand' is the most important element in your promotional bag of tricks.

For more information on branding on the internet, take a look at *Marketing Your Business on the Internet* published by Internet Handbooks. More information on this title can be found at:

http://www.internet-handbooks.co.uk

Learning from internet brands
Consider for a moment some of the internet brands you may have heard of. Your list would probably include some of the following companies:

Amazon	Jungle
AOL	Lastminute
CompuServe	Lycos
Excite	Netscape
Freeserve	Yahoo!

These companies are all new businesses that started with the internet. They have succeeded where their competitors have fared less well. The reason is that each of these firms has a very strong brand. It's a fair bet that you don't even know the physical location of these companies, or the market position they are aiming for. But you do know who they are and what they do – their brand has become established in your mind. This is a far better marketing device than worrying about your location. In fact, it seems that we can use the word web as a new acronym for our modern digital world:

WEB = We Expect Brands

Your viewers expect a branded web site. Without establishing a brand, your web site will not succeed.

Establishing your web site's identity

What does branding mean?

Establishing a brand is more than simply getting people to think of your web site before attempting another. Remember where we get the word 'branding' from. It's the indelible mark that farmers make on livestock in order to identify them. A branding mark on the side of an animal is a quickly recognisable icon for a particular farmer. Associated with this logo is a view about the farmer, how the livestock are kept and so on.

Brands on the internet are similar – they are a recognisable mark that is accompanied by a psychological reaction to it. This reaction is, hopefully, positive. Branding, therefore, can provide you with instant, positive recognition.

The following logos are all familiar to internet users. Simply by looking at them you will have a view about the company and what they do on the internet.

So a brand is a recognisable logo or image that brings to mind some perceptions you have about the company and its products and services. A successful brand is the one that brings with it such a positive view that you do not even stop to consider other brands. This is the nirvana that most web site owners are seeking. However, many web site companies are forgetting a basic fact about branding: time.

Branding is not marketing

Although you clearly need to establish an online brand if your web site is to succeed, do not fall into the trap of thinking that once you have a brand name and logo the job is done – far from it. Brands like Coca Cola, McDonald's, Hewlett Packard and Microsoft all benefit from a common factor: they have been around for a long time.

▶ *Example* – It is all too easy to forget, for example, that Microsoft has been around for almost 30 years, yet only in the past few years – really since the launch of Windows 98 – has it become a 'branded' company. The reason the Microsoft brand has grown so powerful is that the firm has invested considerable time and effort in marketing over a very long period of time. The same is true for Coca Cola, McDonald's, Hewlett Packard and dozens of other brand leaders.

Establishing your web site's identity..............................

In the internet world, the top brands have not had the benefit of time to establish themselves. The world wide web really only began in 1994. However, the top brands have spent considerable sums of money on promotion. What these companies have done is develop a recognisable logo for their branding and then market themselves, using both traditional and online methods. Simply having a logo and a web site is nowhere near enough. Considerable marketing activity is vital if you are to survive in the internet age and your web site is to truly succeed.

Setting up your brand

Before your web site goes live it is a good idea to ensure that you have a logo, or a recognisable image – just like the farmers and their branding irons. Logos do not have to be fancy or cost a great deal. Indeed they do not even need graphics. The Yahoo logo and the Lastminute.com logos are both text-based logos, as are the instantly recognisable logos for Coca Cola and McDonalds, for instance. For help on creating your web site logo go to:

http://www.webreference.com/dlab/

Fig. 1. Dmitry's Design site will help you understand how to produce a stunning corporate identity.

Here you will find plenty of articles on design and how to produce something effective. You will find plenty of logos and other graphic items at:

http://www.clipart.co.uk

You can also buy the book *Creating Logos and Letterheads* from:

http://www.site-promoting.co.uk

Establishing your web site's identity

Fig. 2. Clip Art UK can provide you with a host of designs and ideas for your brand image.

For professional help with branding you could try the Directory of Design Consultants at:

http://www.designdirectory.co.uk/

Here you will find a listing of designers and examples of their work. Naturally, you could also talk to the people who designed your web site, as they may know people who can help with branding. Whichever resource you choose, though, it is important that you develop a brand image which will be quickly and instantly recognisable – just like the Volkswagen VW, the Audi four circles or the McDonald's twin arches. Remember, too, that like these logos your brand image needs to be international, as you are in a global setting on the web.

Branding an established site
If you have an established web site, the first step you need to take is to go through the design and see if you can adapt it so that it becomes branded. It is not a good idea to start promoting your web site until you have a recognisable logo for your brand image. For new web sites, the process of setting up your brand is easy, as no one will have visited your pages yet. For established web sites, the job of branding is more difficult as it may mean your entire web site needs re-designing. However, without considering this, your promotional efforts may well be wasted. Setting up a brand is fundamental to good web site promotion.

Establishing your web site's identity......................................

Choosing the right domain name

Essential to your brand image is your domain name – the name that people will type in to reach you. Many domain names are cumbersome or do not describe what the service on offer at the web site is about. The wrong domain name can seriously dent your image and reduce the value in the brand you are trying to establish. For instance would you rather be known as:

http://www.serviceprovideruk.com/freespace/England/yourname

or

http://www.yourname.co.uk

Clearly, a short, snappy and easy-to-remember name is essential.

Finding advice about domain names
There is plenty of advice on domain names to be found on the internet. You can start your search at:

http://www.name-a.com

If you want to know about domain names
CLICK HERE

If you want to learn more about web site promotion
CLICK HERE

If you want to improve your web safety
CLICK HERE

You can also find the latest news about domain names at:

http://www.domain-name-news.com

You will find more detailed advice on choosing the right domain name in the book, *Naming a Web Site on the Internet*, published by Internet Handbooks (http://www.internet-handbooks.co.uk). Be sure to choose a domain name wisely. The name you choose will have a considerable impact upon your overall image and your chances of promotional success.

Making sure your web site is professional

One of the key factors in achieving success in promoting your web site is your degree of professionalism. The various ways in which you can promote yourself often depend upon people reviewing your pages. If those pages do not look professional they will not get listed in search engines or directories.

A recent survey revealed that one of the key reasons for sites appearing unprofessional is poor text – not bad design. It seems that people are more forgiving of amateurish page design than they are of spelling mistakes or bad grammar. You can find out more details about this survey, and how to make your text professional, at this address:

http://www.the-web-writer.co.uk

.... **Establishing your web site's identity**

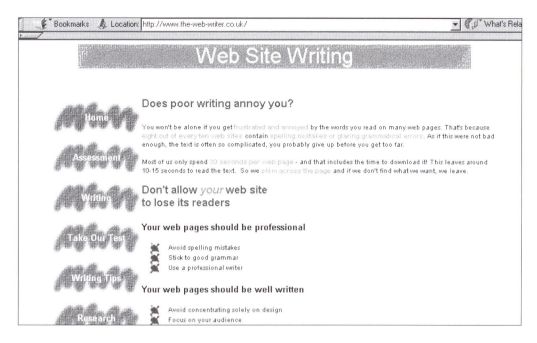

Fig. 3. The Web Writer can ensure your web site text is at its best.

Developing a professional design
Of course, this does not mean your web site should have amateurish pages with brilliant text! The design, too, needs to be professional. You can gain more information on how to improve your design at:

http://info.med.yale.edu/caim/manual/

This site is the Yale Style Manual and offers an excellent guide to web design. You can also discover plenty of useful tips in the book *Building a Web Site on the Internet*, available from Internet Handbooks at:

http://www.internet-handbooks.co.uk

Ensuring your systems are robust

The professional look and feel of your web site is one sure way of boosting your promotional capability. However, you will soon lose out on any web site promotion if you are not set up to cope with the flood of emails you will receive from:

1. site indexing organisations
2. search engines
3. link generators

Your chances of promotion will go downhill if you do not have businesslike arrangements for dealing with email and other requests for information. You may also need a database to store username details for the many sites you will use for promoting your own web pages.

Establishing your web site's identity

It is essential that you have some system in place at the outset if you are to cope. If you do not establish a database, and a system for dealing with all the enquiries you will generate, you will lose out in all kinds of valuable promotional opportunities.

Promotional follow-up

Your chances of promoting your site will be considerably extended if your follow up systems are professional. One of the reasons for this is that search engines will sometimes rank you according to the number of links you have on other sites. People will only choose to link to your site if it looks really professional. A good follow-up system that engenders a positive image of your web site will tend to lead to increased links and therefore higher placement within search engine lists. As an example, consider the case of Intersaver:

Intersaver
http://www.intersaver.co.uk
This company provides a whole host of electrical and home goods at lower prices than high street stores. Like many web sites, Intersaver promoted its services but an eagle-eyed reader found a number of mistakes in the company's advertising. As a result, Intersaver received an email that said they really should make sure their advertising was accurate, otherwise the service may not be trusted.

That email was sent on a Saturday and Intersaver's managing director, John Thornhill replied on the Sunday morning. He said:

> 'Thanks very much for the input – as far as we're aware you're the first person to have noticed the error. We really appreciate customer feedback and to express our gratitude we would be pleased to offer you a further 5% discount on your first purchase at Intersaver. I have already arranged for the advertising to be corrected. Best Wishes. John.'

Such an effective means of rapid reply, with a positive answer, is what you need to ensure your web site gains a good reputation. With a positive reputation you will receive more links. The more links you have around the web, the greater your ranking in search engine directories, which in turn will lead to more of those valuable hits, and even greater success. Without an effective follow-up system in place, your web site could suffer from a bad reputation as well as a lower placing in search engines.

The secrets of successful planning

The excitement at producing your own web site, or contributing to a large business site, should not blind you to the essential tasks you need to perform if your promotional efforts are not to be wasted. Here are six key steps. You need to:

1. Establish a brand.
2. Choose a memorable logo.

Establishing your web site's identity

3. Register the right domain name.
4. Ensure your text is professional.
5. Check your design thoroughly.
6. Set up efficient follow-up systems.

Only when you have done all this will you really be in a position to start promoting your site. There is clearly a lot of work to do before you can generate those much sought-after page 'hits'. Throughout the web you will find articles and information about promotion. Many of them reiterate the points made in this chapter. In short, far too many people needlessly limit the value of their sites and the accompanying promotion because they fail to pay sufficient attention to the basics.

2 Getting listed in search engines

In this chapter we will explore:

▶ *making your pages 'search engine friendly'*
▶ *using meta tag analysis software*
▶ *meta tags and frames*
▶ *making your pages acceptable to search engines*
▶ *submitting your site to search engines*
▶ *submitting your site manually*
▶ *using automatic submission services*
▶ *using software to submit your site*
▶ *repeating your submission*
▶ *reviewing the search-engine submission process*

Without some means of finding pages on the world wide web, the internet would be very difficult to use. That's why a number of 'search engines' have been developed to help you find what you want. In a sense, these search engines are a bit like an interactive telephone directory that allows you to find just what you are looking for, with just a fragment of information. In fact, a search engine is just an easy-to-use database, albeit complex 'behind the scenes'.

One of the mistakes often made by newcomers to the internet is believing that the search engines list everything that is available. They do not. Search engines are commercial enterprises which make their money from advertising and a range of support services. As such, the main search engines choose what to index, based upon their market. This means you can find something listed in one search engine that is not listed at another competing system.

There is no single complete index to the internet. That is frustrating for users, but it also poses a problem for people who own or run web sites. Your potential viewers will be using a variety of search engines. For this reason you need to get listed in all of them (or as many as you possibly can), otherwise some people will not be able to find you or even know about your site. Indeed, research published in the leading science journal *Nature* showed that search engines index 16 per cent or less of the entire web.[1] You can find more details about this research at:

http://www.wwwmetrics.com/

Each of the search engine companies has different reasons for including (or not including) web sites or web pages in their directory. They reject many web pages that don't make the grade. To make sure yours gets included, you will need to work hard at ensuring that all the details of your submission are right. One minor mistake means you will not be listed. You will become part of that vast twilight zone of 84 per cent of web pages that are simply never indexed.

---

1 *Nature*, 1999, 400, 107–109

Getting listed in search engines

Making your pages 'search engine friendly'

Before you even consider submitting your site for listing at a particular search engine, make quite sure that your pages meet the criteria for inclusion. Each of the top search engines has its own specific standards, which are discussed in the next chapter, but they share one common requirement: the use of 'meta tags'. Without these items of code, a search engine will not index your web site. You absolutely must include them in your web site page.

If another company, or someone other than yourself, has designed your pages, make sure that they include meta tags in the coding of the pages. If you designed your web site yourself, go back to each page and insert the necessary codes. This is an essential task and will pay off handsomely in the future.

Using meta tags

A meta tag is a special small piece of code inserted into each web page. It is invisible to the viewer but can be seen by search engine indexing programs known as 'spiders' or 'crawlers'. These are programs that scour the web for page information and report back to the search engines, saying what the code includes. The search engine can then use your meta tags in its database system. When someone searches for a word that matches one of your meta tags, your web site will appear in a list of potential sites that may be of use to the individual undertaking the search. Without meta tags the search engine would have to index your entire web site.

Although many search engines do this, others do not. Meta tags therefore allow you to control the words that the search engine will index. However, search engines always look at the actual text in your pages, though some will not index it. If they find that your meta tags do not match your web site text, your pages will be rejected from indexing.

▶ *Example* – One of the most searched for terms in the year 2000 has been 'Britney Spears' (the teenage pop star). If you made these words into meta tags, but your web site did not include those words in the actual text, your site would be rejected. Meta tags must match your web site, otherwise the search engine will reject you. This underlines the importance of your web site text itself – provided this is well written and to the point, it will be easy for search engines to index your pages and provide you with more hits.

Although meta tags are very important, you should not be lulled into a false sense of security – they in no way replace a good, well-written, well-designed web site. Even so, you would be daft not to include meta tags in your web pages, since they help the indexing process.

Inserting meta tags into your page
Your meta tags are pieces of hypertext mark-up language code (HTML), which is the computer program used to create all web pages. Most web design programs allow you to view the code and some allow you to edit it

Getting listed in search engines

as well. You can insert meta tags manually if you have access to the raw code for your page. Programs such as HotMetal and Microsoft FrontPage allow you to do this. So too does Adobe GoLive and Macromedia Dreamweaver. Essentially, to alter HTML code directly you need a professional level web design program.

All meta tags are inserted after the codes that indicate the page heading and the main part of the page – the head and body tags. These look like this:

```
<HEAD>
</HEAD>
<BODY>
```

Your meta tags must go between the two head tags, otherwise they will not work. There are a variety of meta tags you can use, but two essential ones are the 'description' tag and the 'keywords' tag. These should be entered as follows:

```
<HEAD>
<META NAME="description" content="your description here">
<META NAME="keywords" content="your keywords here">
</HEAD>
<BODY>
```

The 'description' tag is your chosen description of your web site and will be used by some search engines when they display your site in a list for people making a search. The keywords are the words that you think people would use to search for information that is within your site.

As you can see, entering a description and a series of keywords is comparatively straightforward and can result in your pages being properly indexed by search engines.

Adding a title tag

Another HTML tag that you should use is the 'title'. This is not strictly a meta tag, but works in much the same way. A title tag is the one that a search engine will use in the list of pages it displays to viewers; if your page title is simply 'Home Page' this will not help viewers decide whether to visit you, no matter how enticing your description meta tag. If your title says 'Visit us for free travel advice' you are more likely to get your viewers. Once again, though, the text of your site must reflect the content of your title tag, otherwise it will not be accepted by the search engine. For instance, there is no value in using a title tag that is simply 'Sex, Sex, Sex' and then have on your front page 'Good, now that we have your attention let's talk about embroidery'.

To insert a title tag all you need type is:

```
<TITLE>Your page title here</TITLE>
```

This must appear between the two head tags:

Getting listed in search engines

```
<HEAD>
<TITLE>Your page title here</TITLE>
</HEAD>
```

The usual convention is to **place the title tag before any meta tags,** as this helps speed up indexing. The combination of a title tag and meta tags can make your site much more search engine friendly. The example below is from The Web Writer (http://www.the-web-writer.co.uk). You can see that there are many other meta tags, all of which help the search engine include you and locate you.

```
<html>

<head>
<meta http-equiv="Content-Type" content="text/html; charset=windows-1252">
<meta http-equiv="Content-Language" content="en-us">
<title>Writing Professional Web Site Text . . The Web Writer</title>
<meta name="GENERATOR" content="Microsoft FrontPage 4.0">
<meta name="ProgId" content="FrontPage.Editor.Document">
<meta name="description" content="The Web Writer is full of free advice and support to help you make your web site more professional. We ensure there are no errors or spelling mistakes and that your pages have good grammar and a style that helps your reader. We can assess your current site for free and then re-write or produce your text professionally.">
<meta name="keywords" content="write, writer, writing, web, Web, WebSite, web site, net, Net, Internet, internet, professional, spelling, grammar, text, editing, design, designers, site, mistake, good, reader, audience, assess, test, free, bookshop, articles, research, tips, writing tips, news, credentials, assessment, annoy, error, web page, page, skim, style, consistency, improvements, design, you, advice, support, re-write, keyword">
<meta name="robots" content="index, follow">
<meta name="revisit-after" content="30">
<meta name="author" content="Graham Jones">
<meta name="copyright" content="The Web Adviser">
<meta name="reply-to" content="graham@the-web-adviser.co.uk">
<meta name="language" content="en-gb">
<meta name="classification" content="Internet Services">
<meta name="distribution" content="Global">
<meta name="Microsoft Theme" content="canvas 010">
</head>

<body>
```

Getting listed in search engines ....

Fig. 4. Cyber Eye Web Site Promotion is a useful resource for understanding meta tags and how they can improve search engine position.

Finding out more
You can find out more about using meta tags at CyberEye at:

http://www.meta-tags.com

Automating the meta tag process
If you are wary about manually inserting meta tags, you can always get a program to do it for you! Naturally enough there are plenty of automated meta-tag generators available. The one you choose will depend on your personal preferences, price, and how the program integrates with your current web-design program.

Fig. 5. Webs Unlimited make MetaTag Maker for Microsoft FrontPage 2000.

Getting listed in search en~

For instance, if you use Microsoft FrontPage there is an add-on you can buy called MetaTag Maker. This is produced by Webs Unlimited at:

http://www.websunlimited.com/

You can download this add-in direct from the site at $34.95. For FrontPage users this is money well spent. If you want to try it before you buy it there is a demonstration version available as well.

If you do not have Microsoft FrontPage all is not lost. You can use a web-based service to produce the meta tags for you. Go to:

http://www.submitcorner.com/Tools/Meta/

Here you can produce your meta tags by following the instructions you receive on screen. All you then have to do is copy and paste the resulting tags into your web page.

If you would rather use a separate program on your own PC to generate the meta tags there plenty to choose from. You can find a list and download them from SoftSeek at:

http://www.softseek.com/Internet/Web_Publishing_Tools/HTML_META_Tag_Tools/

One of the most popular programs for generating meta tags is Metabot. You can download a trial version of this from the publishers, Watchfire, at:

http://www.tetranetsoftware.com/products/metabot.htm

Fig. 6. SubmitIt Corner has a meta tag generator to help produce your essential tags.

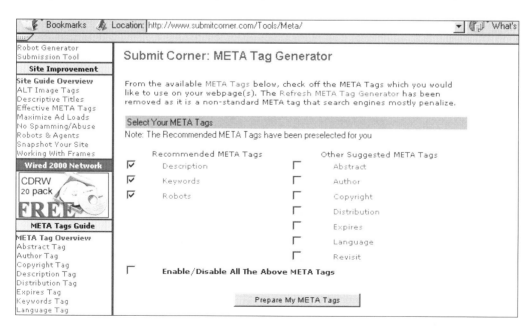

25

in search engines

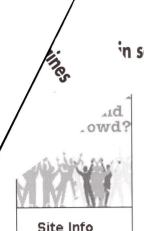

Site Info

First Time Visit? Click Here!

See What's New!

Search Engine Headlines

This program allows you to produce all the meta tags you need and will insert them automatically for you. If you want to learn more about meta tags and find out what they can and cannot achieve, you should go to Search Engine Watch:

Search Engine Watch
http://www.searchenginewatch.com/webmasters/meta.html
This web page provides a great deal of in-depth information and links to a host of resources about meta tags.

Analysing your meta tags
Once you have inserted your meta tags you need to analyse them to make sure they will be effective. Your analysis should start with spell checking – print out the HTML code and proofread the tags you have inserted. A spelling error could mean your page is not indexed or is hard to find. Misspelt tags are a common problem that can cause difficulties for search engines. You should also compare the keyword tags you have inserted with the text on the web page itself. Do your keywords actually appear on the page? If so, how frequently? The more often a tag keyword appears on a page, the greater your chances of being indexed – but don't include words like 'the' or 'and' as these will be rejected by the search engines which are really only interested in nouns and verbs. If all this analytical work seems tedious, you can get software to help and to report back to you on what you should do.

Using meta tag analysis software

If you have bought an add-in program for your web creation program, it will almost certainly include spell checking and basic analysis. Some of the stand-alone meta tag generator programs also include analysis tools. One of the best analysis tools, though, is the Page Critic portion of Web Position Gold.

Web Position Gold
http://www.webpositiongold.com/
This program has a range of options from producing meta tags right through to submitting your site to a search engine. However one of the main features is the meta tag analysis section. This part of the program provides a full analysis of your meta tags and advises you on what to change for each particular search engine. This is phenomenal power and it is no wonder that Web Position Gold is one of the most widely recommended programs for helping to achieve improved indexing for web sites. You can find out more about Web Position Gold and download a trial from here.

Hi-Verify Slide Show
requires IE4 or higher
Hi-Verify™

Screen Shots
Hi-Verify™

Download
Hi-Verify™

Support

Hi-Verify
http://www.hisoftware.com/verify.htm
Another popular program is Hi-Verify. You can find out more about this here. This program comes in a variety of formats from a stand-alone 'full' edition, to add-ons for various web site creation programs. Using this

Getting listed in search engines

program provides an in-depth analysis of your meta tags and explanations of what you need to do to improve your site.

Submit Corner
http://www.submitcorner.com/
If you would rather use web-based tools for analysing your meta tags one is based at Submit Corner. You can find this here. All you have to do is enter your web site address (its URL) and you quickly get a report back showing you what you need to do to improve your meta tags. This is a quick and easy service and may be all you need. However, for a more thorough analysis of your meta tags you may need a meta tag 'expert' to go through your pages to check them. You can order such a service for $50 from Submit-URL at:

http://www.submit-url.net/services.htm#Expert Site Evaluation

Fig. 7. Web Position Gold is an excellent tool to help you analyse your site and improve its chances of being indexed by search engines.

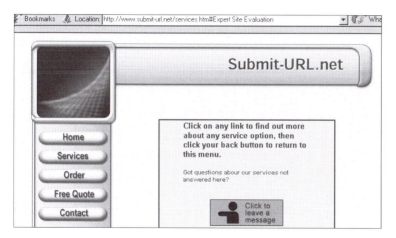

Fig. 8. Submit-URL can check your site to make sure it is likely to gain high placement in search engines.

27

Getting listed in search engines ....

There is a free checking service at Microsoft B-Central:

http://www.bcentral.com/

The SubmitIt service has a meta tag checking and creation tool.

ProBoost
http://www.proboost.com/
You might also like to try ProBoost. This charges a monthly fee from $49.99 but is an extensive service offering live 24-hour support.

NetMechanic
http://www.netmechanic.com
Another useful checking service is NetMechanic. Although this does not check meta tags for suitability, the site does check that your coding is correct. It also ensures that all your links work. One of the reasons why search engines can reject sites from their lists is poor coding and non-operating links. NetMechanic offers a free check as well as a more in-depth analysis at $35.

Whichever route you choose to analyse your tags and your code, it is an essential task prior to submitting your web site to a search engine. Significant numbers of sites are rejected from the indexing process because of this lack of attention to detail.

Meta tags and frames

Meta tags work well with all kinds of web site designs, except those that use frames. Frames are devices that essentially allow you to show several different web pages on screen at the same time. This means, for instance, your left-hand column, or frame, can show a contents list that remains in place while the right-hand frame can show varied material. In this way

Fig. 9. NetMechanic will check your web site to make sure it works properly.

Getting listed in search engines

you can retain a consistent look and feel about your web site and make navigation easier. It also means the site can be faster to use as viewers only have to update a single frame, with all the other material on view remaining in place. This means it does not have to be downloaded, thus speeding up the page.

Frames also have other advantages, since you can include other web sites within your own. This means that you can arrange links to appear in a particular frame, rather than replacing the whole page. That way you can keep people within your web site, rather than losing them. Frames therefore have tremendous advantages.

However, frames have some serious disadvantages. For a start, not all web browsers are capable of displaying them properly. As a result, a proportion of your viewers may not be able to view your site. You can overcome this by having a non-framed site for people who haven't upgraded their browsers, but this means your development time is increased and you need more web space at your hosting company to accommodate what is really two web sites.

The problem of indexing
The most serious problem for people who like to use frames on their web sites is the difficulty that search engines have in indexing. Just which frame should they index? If you include meta tags in each frame they will not necessarily achieve anything.

▶ *Example* – Suppose you have a navigation bar in a frame that is repeated on every page. Such bars rarely have any associated text, so the search engine will have nothing to index. The search engine will not necessarily be able to see your main frame and so your site will be rejected.

Since meta tags are so important in promoting your web site, you should avoid frames at all costs. If your site is frames-based, the best way to make sure it is properly listed in search engines using meta tags is to scrap the design and produce a new version not based on frames.

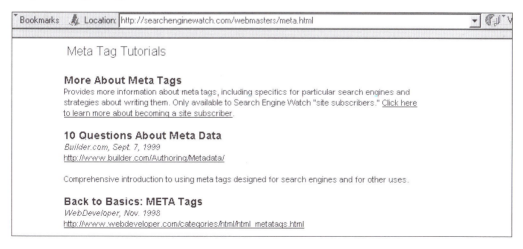

Getting listed in search engines

▶ *Tip* – If you are using frames in order to keep people within your site when you link to other pages, the best way to do this is to use pop up windows with JavaScript code. You can find out how to achieve this at: http://grahamjones.net/java.htm

Making your pages acceptable to search engines

There are just a few steps you need to take to make sure that your page is suitable for indexing by all the search engines. Even though there are some differences in the way they index web sites, each of the search engines share a great deal of common ground.

1. Get rid of any frames. Design your web page using straightforward techniques.

2. Insert a strong title tag that succinctly states what your web page does.

3. Add meta tags to describe your pages and the keywords people might use to search for you.

4. Check your web site text and make sure the keywords you have used as meta tags appear frequently on the page itself.

5. Analyse your meta tags to make sure they are spelled correctly and are within recommended parameters.

By performing these tasks you will be ready to submit to the various search engines.

Page design tips to help improve listing in search engines

(a) Avoid web sites that need registration or passwords.

(b) Avoid publishing databases – convert them into standard web HTML first.

(c) Avoid 'Active Server Pages' – they are unlikely to be indexed.

(d) Avoid dynamic pages – they will not be indexed.

(e) Do not use scanned graphics of text (such as your company brochure) as graphics cannot be indexed.

(f) Keep your pages small – some indexing services will time out if you have complex pages.

(g) Put your most important information at the top of each page, with the absolutely most vital material on the first page.

(h) Have plenty of links – to other pages in your web site and to external sites. Search engines like you to have lots of links.

Getting listed in search engines

Submitting your site to search engines

There are three main ways you can submit your pages to search engines. These are manual submission, automatic submission, and third party submission. As you go from the top to the bottom of this list you lose control, but you gain time.

▶ *Manual submission* – This is laborious and very slow, but you decide exactly how your site will be submitted and how you want it to be listed.

▶ *Automatic transmission* – This means you either use a computer program or a web-based service to send your site to several search engines at the same time. This makes it faster for you, but you cannot be as specific about your entry as you might like.

▶ *Third party submissions* – Are those which you handover to someone else. There are many companies offering submission services. You simply tell them your web site address and they do the rest. You have to trust them, but your submission process is very quick indeed.

Which method you select will depend on how much time you have available and how much money you can afford for software or third party submission services. However, there is nothing yet that can beat the manual submission to each search engine where you are in total control. If you have the time available – and you will need a day or two – this is the best option.

Submitting your site manually

To submit your site manually you need to visit each of the search engines one at a time and follow their instructions for suggesting a new site they may like to index. The main reason for refusing a site is that these directions are not adhered to properly. One of the principal reasons for the instructions is the way in which the search engine indexes web sites. They use automatic software for much of the work – called a crawler, or a spider or sometimes a robot. These programs can only work properly if they have the right material to work with. The directives at each search engine ensure that their robot software will be able to properly index your site. Failure to follow the instructions will mean your site may not be indexed and therefore will not be listed. To ensure your site is properly listed, stick to the instructions to the letter!

Using automatic submission services

If you do not want to go through the laborious process of submitting your site to each search engine, one at a time, there are two kinds of automated service available:

1. Software that you can buy to perform the task.

Getting listed in search engines

2. Web-based services that will submit on your behalf.

The choice you make will depend on how much control you wish to retain. If you buy software you will have to enter many of the details necessary and choose the search engines to which you wish to submit. If you use web-based services, you will not usually get a choice of search engines, though the details you need to complete will be fewer.

Using software to submit your site

There is a wide variety of site submission software that varies from cheap 'shareware' to full blown commercial products. Some programs only submit to the main search engines, others submit to hundreds. For a good selection of different programs, including many trials of commercial products, go to SoftSeek at:

http://www.softseek.com/Internet/Web_Publishing_Tools/Search_Engine_Submission_Tools/

Here you will discover over 75 different site submission programs from the simple to the sophisticated. You can take your pick! SoftSeek includes some of the major programs that are used widely. These include:

Fig. 10. A good selection of search engine submission software can be found at SoftSeek.

> Exploit Submission Wizard
> PageSubmit Pro
> Submit Wolf Pro
> Traffic Builder
> Web Position Gold

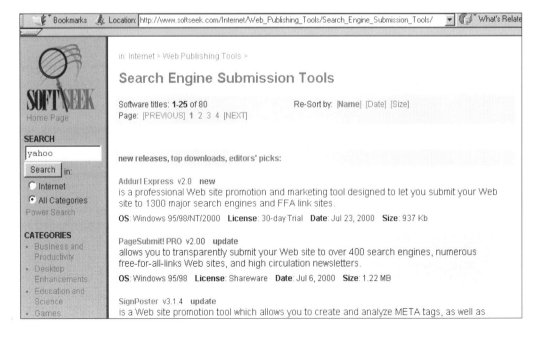

Getting listed in search engines

Each of these programs has different strengths and weaknesses; as with many computer programs, personal choice will play a significant part. Some people just love one of these programs, but hate another, whereas others think the complete reverse! Because most of them are comparatively small programs, you can easily download a few and try them all out. However, the five listed here always get rave reviews, so it may be worth starting with them first, before you tackle the other 70!

Exploit Submission Wizard
http://www.exploit.net/wizard/index.html
This program can submit your web site to 400 different search engines. You can find out full details about the program at the address above. The program can be updated so that you are submitting to the latest search engines with the most recent recommendations. This is an attractive feature as it helps ensure your submissions will be accurate. However, to use this feature you need to purchase a 'software key', which is time-limited. You can get an annual key for £90. Even so, this may be well worth it as the program is easy to use and provides complete reports on the success – or otherwise – of your submission.

Fig. 11. Exploit Submission Wizard can help get your site listed on hundreds of search engines, including the all-important main sites.

Page Submit Pro
http://www.pagesubmit.com
Page Submit Pro can complete all those 'add URL' forms automatically for you, thus saving time. You can find out more details at the address above. One of the advantages of PageSubmit Pro is that it includes the ability to submit your site to newsletters as well as search engines. Often people

Getting listed in search engines

Fig. 12. Page Submit Pro has a range of features including the ability to automatically fill in the 'add URL' forms of the major search engines.

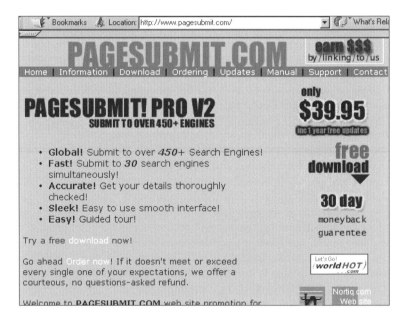

find out about sites from newsletters, so this is an excellent additional advantage. Also, this is a British program and includes the UK-based search engines, which many of the other programs do not. For instance, there are different categories in Yahoo! UK from those in Yahoo!. Hence it is worth submitting to these British search engines separately.

Fig. 13. Submit Wolf Pro can get you listed at over 1,500 different search engines.

Submit Wolf Pro
http://www.trellian.com/swolf/index.html
Submit Wolf Pro can get you listed at over 1,500 different places on the

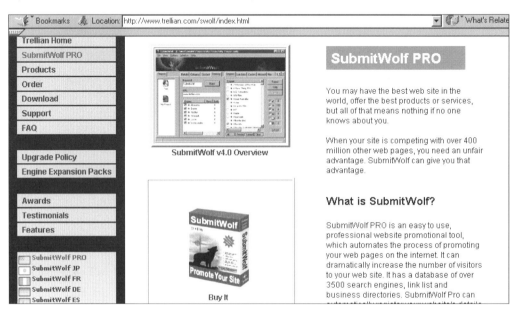

Getting listed in search engines

web. You can check out the details of the program here. This web site boasts that there have been more than one million copies of this program downloaded, making it a very popular tool indeed. You will also discover from this web site that over 1,000 of the web-based submission services actually use Submit Wolf Pro to do their job. Also, some of these services make a charge for each web site you want to promote. If you have more than one, you'll have to pay additional fees. With Submit Wolf Pro, you only pay for the program once and then you can submit as many different web site addresses as you like. You get a complete and in-depth report on your submissions and the ability to track progress. This is altogether an excellent package.

Traffic Builder
http://www.intelliquis.com/products/traffic.stm
This program allows you to submit your site to an amazing 3,500 search engines. However, many of the search engines are highly specialist. There are some you may not wish to send your web site to, such as 'XXX Fantasy Movies Post' which is included in the list. This means you will have to scroll down a long list to select each individual search engine you want to reach. Many of them are obscure and you may need to research them before deciding whether or not to submit to them.

In essence, Traffic Builder is not much different from the other submission programs, except for its huge list of target sites. This can work against you, as it may take you longer to sort through this list than to manually submit your web site to the major search engines. Still, if you want absolute maximum coverage, this product is excellent; you could not possibly submit to all these search engines (even if you knew about them) in the short time that Traffic Builder takes to complete the task. You can find out more at the address shown above.

Fig. 14. Traffic Builder can be downloaded direct from this web site so you can try it before buying it.

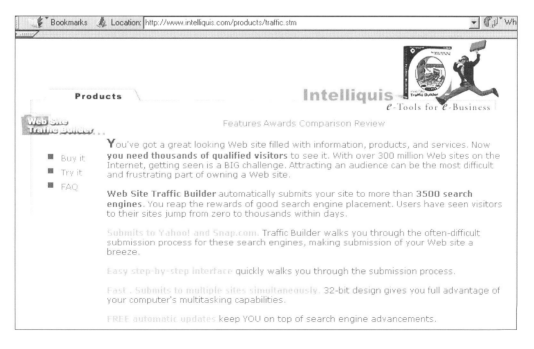

35

Getting listed in search engines ....

Web Position Gold
http://www.webposition.com
This program concentrates on the leading search engines, ignoring the minor ones completely. The argument for this is that over 80 per cent of all searches are conducted at a handful of leading sites. For this reason, Web Position Gold is much more than a site submitter. Instead, the program is designed to help you maximise your success in achieving a high ranking within each of the main search engines. As such the program helps to write meta tags, gives advice on how to improve your site, and even helps to construct doorway or gateway pages – new home pages that act as an entry point to your site and include all the essential items of text and meta tags to ensure high listings on the search engines. Full details about this powerful program are available at the site.

Using web services to submit your site

There are several web-based services that will submit your site. Many of them use software that you could buy yourself to do the task. However, you will save time by filling in one form online and then letting the web service to do the rest of the work for you. There are literally hundreds of web-based submission services. You can find a list of several at:

http://online-biz.com/promote/

Submit It
http://submitit.bcentral.com/
One of the most popular online submission services, though, is that run by Microsoft, called Submit It. You can find this service here. It provides a check of your web site, an analysis of your meta tags, and can selectively submit your URL to various categories of search engines. The service is

Fig. 15. Online Biz provides a comprehensive list of links to companies that can submit your web site to search engines for you.

Check out these sites	for...
Affiliate Central	Free submission to over 3000+FFA Sites
Announce-O-Matic	Free submission to 300 Search engines, Classifieds, & FFA Links
Award Submit	Free submission to 100's of Awards sites
Business Heaven	Free submission to over 1800 Search Engines and links pages
Business Web	Free submission to 22 search engines
Cyber Mall	Free submission to over 3500+ Links Pages
Ebookz	Free submission to 3000 Search Engines
Elite Concepts	Free submission to over 750 Search Engines and Directories
E-Marketing FFA	Free submission to over 400 FFA links pages
E-Marketing Classifieds	Free submission to over 400 classified ad sites

Getting listed in search engines

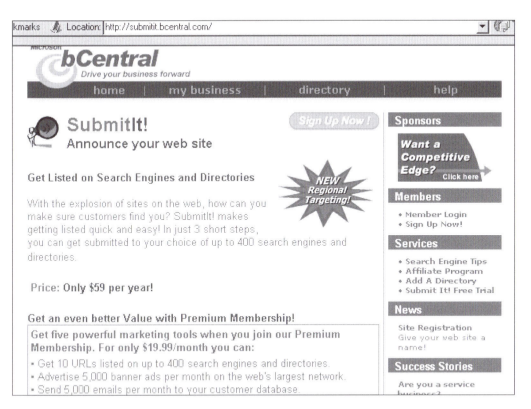

Fig. 16. Submit It from Microsoft can help you get your site listed in a host of different search engines.

not fully automatic, though. Instead, the various forms are completed for you and you are then taken through a series of screens to check that the information is correct and to add any details required by specific search engines. This is quite slow when compared with other web-based submission services, but it is more thorough. Even so, the Submit It service is likely to be a much faster process than you would be faced with on your own.

Repeating your submission

No matter which method you use to submit your site to search engines, the key thing to remember is that you need to keep doing it! If your page is not re-indexed regularly by some search engines it will be removed. Equally important are the changes you will be making to your web site. Every time you alter your web site, you need to resubmit – the search engines will only be as good as the index they have. If your web site is changed, an old index might not find you. That's why you need to con- stantly re-submit. However, some search engines will delete you from their index if you submit too frequently!

Follow the advice that each search engine provides. Generally, you will find that resubmitting every month or two is not usually frowned upon. You can arrange meta tags to do this automatically if you wish, though some search engines will ignore this request. Web-based services and software can be set up to ensure periodic resubmission, and your site will benefit if you take advantage of this.

Getting listed in search engines ....

Reviewing the search engine submission process

No matter what you do with your web site, you need placement on the search engines. If you can get your web site listed by the Top 12, you'll receive significant traffic, since these search engines are responsible for the vast majority of searches on the internet.

However, there are thousands of other search engines from which you could benefit. Provided you have a good, well-written site, with appropriate meta tags, and you use some professional support in the form of software or a web service, your site should gain a respectable position in the search engine listings. Without attention to detail, though, your site will not receive many hits, as it might not get listed at all or it could be buried in a long list of thousands.

Achieving maximum coverage
To achieve maximum coverage you need to:

1. Produce a professional and well-written web site.

2. Make your site search-engine friendly.

3. Use good meta tags.

4. Submit your site using some professional support.

5. Re-submit your site regularly.

Visit the free Internet HelpZone at
www.internet-handbooks.co.uk
Helping you master the internet

---

3 Applying to the top search engines

In this chapter we will explore:

- *AltaVista*
- *Ask Jeeves*
- *Excite*
- *Google*
- *HotBot*
- *Infoseek*
- *LookSmart*
- *Lycos*
- *MSN*
- *Scrub The Web*
- *Snap*
- *Webcrawler*
- *Yahoo!*

Of the several hundred search engines, there is a group of a baker's dozen that are the most popular. These receive by far the greatest majority of searches that people make on the internet. The remaining search engines are mostly specialist, searching, say, for sites in a particular country or on a specific topic. For example, there is an airport search engine that allows you to find pages on the web related to airports:

http://www.uni-karlsruhe.de/~un9v/atm/ase.html

Many other equally specialist search engines exist. For most people with web sites, though, the aim is to get listed on the major search engines in the 'Top 13'. The leading ones to target are:

AltaVista	Ask Jeeves	Excite
Google	HotBot	Infoseek
LookSmart	Lycos	MSN
Scrub The Web	Snap	Webcrawler
Yahoo!		

AltaVista

AltaVista is one of the biggest search engines and is jointly owned by the internet conglomerate CMGI and the computer manufacturing giant Compaq. Originally AltaVista was owned by the Digital Equipment Corporation and produced the first ever index of web sites in 1995. Nowadays AltaVista is a significant player in search technology, owning 60 patents in this field and boasting the fastest search engine on the web. Its main home page is at:

http://www.altavista.com

Applying to the top search engines ....

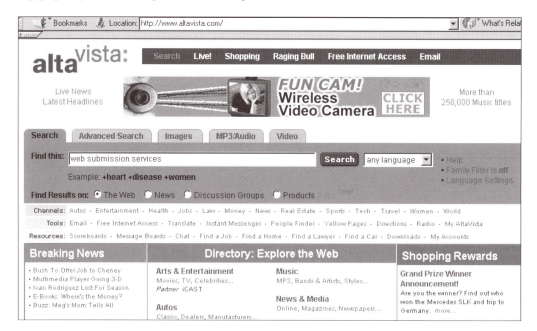

Fig. 17. AltaVista is one of the largest search engines on the web.

You can check how AltaVista compares with the competition by visiting Search Engine Watch at:

http://www.searchenginewatch.com

It provides detailed statistics and information about search engines. In fact for anyone who wants to promote a web site, Search Engine Watch is an essential resource. Here you will find that AltaVista is indeed a popular search engine attracting considerable usage. You will want cer-

Fig. 18. Search Engine Watch will show you comparisons of the various search engines.

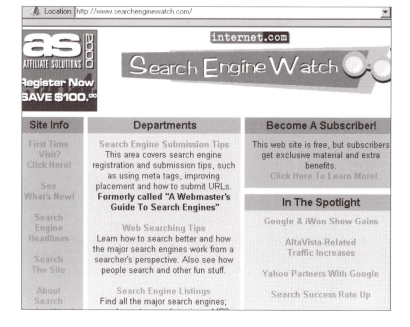

Applying to the top search engines

tainly want to be listed here. To add your web site go to:

http://www.uni-karlsruhe.de/~un9v/atm/ase.html

Next, click on Add a URL which you will find under AltaVista Business Solutions, half way down the left side of the screen. Simply type in the complete web site address, e.g. http://www.internet-handbooks.co.uk, and press the Submit button. Your page will then be indexed and added to the list for processing. This means your page will be checked and then inserted into the AltaVista index provided it meets the company's criteria. Reasons why you may not be included are clearly stated on the web site submission page of AltaVista.

Provided you follow the rules, AltaVista has one of the easiest submission processes and one of the fastest indexing services. Your page will be indexed straight away after you have pressed the Submit button.

Ask Jeeves

Ask Jeeves is a 'natural language' search engine, which means you can type in questions to which you want an answer. The search engine then goes away and comes back with a series of categorised answers for you. The company began offering search services in 1997 following the formation of Ask Jeeves by a venture capitalist and a software engineer. Its main home page is at:

http://www.askjeeves.com

A real person reviews every page that is indexed by Ask Jeeves. They don't use robots and spiders; they actually visit your site and see whether or not it fits within their editorial guidelines. To get your site reviewed and

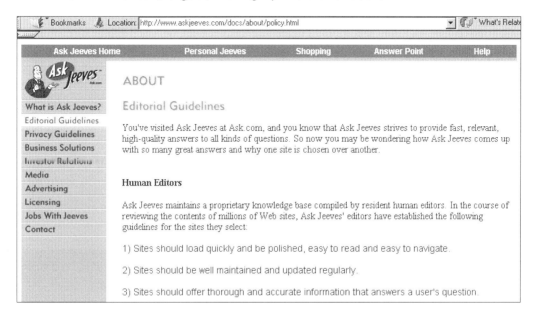

Fig. 19. Ask Jeeves is a simple-looking site with a whole host of search resources behind it.

Applying to the top search engines

included you need to send an email to:

url@ask.com

State in your message that you want your web site considered and they will do the rest. You can find the editorial guidelines at Ask Jeeves here:

http://www.askjeeves.com/docs/about/policy.html

Excite

Excite is a significant player in the world of search engines. It began life, like many American high-tech companies, with a group of college guys hanging out in their garage. It took two and a half years of work and plenty of phone calls and meetings before Excite was born at the end of 1995. Since then, Excite has expanded and has even bought out some of its competition. It is now one of the main search engines on the internet. Its main home page is at:

http://www.excite.com

Adding your web site is easy. Just go to:

http://www.excite.co.uk/info/add_url

Enter your web site address and your email address and the rest is done by Excite. You will find a series of hints and tips on improving your chances of success at the help pages of Excite at:

http://www.excite.co.uk/info/help

Fig. 20. Excite's UK search engine provides a range of add-on options and can be personalised by the viewer.

Applying to the top search engines

Fig. 21. You can easily add your web site to Google at this web page.

Google

Google is an unusual search engine, in that the list of pages it provides in response to a particular user's search is based on the number of links that the pages have received. So, the more people who have links to your site, the higher up the Google list you will go. If no one has links to your site, you may not even get listed by Google, or you'll be at the bottom of the list. The theory behind Google is that the more people who link to you, the more web sites there are that think you are worthwhile. In order to get the best out of Google, therefore, you need to ensure that as many people as possible link to your site. This is covered in more detail in Chapter 6. Google's main home page is at:

   http://www.google.com

Ensuring you get lots of links will help your ranking in the Google searches, but it is more important than this. Google technology is employed by Yahoo!, the search engine used by almost half of the world's surfers. Hence a good placing in Google will work wonders for your listing in Yahoo! To add your web site to Google go to:

   http://www.google.com/addurl.html

HotBot

HotBot is part of Lycos, another major search engine. The difference between the two engines is largely in the way they appear to the viewer. HotBot is a quick, direct search engine with no extra fancy features. Lycos, on the other hand, has a range of additional features that viewers

Applying to the top search engines

Fig. 22. HotBot is part of the Lycos network, but you should still submit your site separately to the HotBot pages.

can utilise. The main home page of HotBot is at:

http://www.hotbot.com

To submit your site to HotBot, go to the web site address shown above and click on the Submit Web Site button. To find out how to improve your site so that it gains higher ranking in the HotBot lists go to:

http://hotbot.lycos.com/help/addurl/#13

There are two key factors which will prevent your site from being indexed by HotBot.

1. Your site must not require cookies.

2. Your site must not exceed 50 pages.

Provided you stick to these rules, and the general guidelines on preparing web sites for search engines, you should gain a listing in HotBot.

InfoSeek

InfoSeek is run by Go.com, a new company set up by InfoSeek, the Disney Corporation and Buena Vista. Its main home page is at:

http://www.infoseek.com

Like Ask Jeeves, the InfoSeek site allows you to use 'natural language' questions to find what you need. However, it is not as responsive. For instance, if you ask 'How do I add my URL?' at AskJeeves, the first item returned is a link to a page of instructions. Over at InfoSeek, the same

Applying to the top search engines

Fig. 23. InfoSeek is a simple site that allows for quick and easy searches.

question produces over 700 possible links. This does not bode well for the search capability of InfoSeek. In fact, you can easily find details about adding your web site by clicking on the Tips button on the main home page of InfoSeek. Here you can access the submission page, which is at:

http://www.infoseek.com/AddUrl?pg=DCaddurl.html&sv=UK

You enter your web site address then click on the submit button and then you are returned to the home page. You don't even get a thank you or any kind of confirmation that your site will be checked. You simply have to trust InfoSeek to do something. Happily, even though InfoSeek is one of the Top 13 web search engines, it is not at the top of the list – that place is still held by Yahoo!.

LookSmart

LookSmart is a significant player in the search engine market because it provides searching facilities for a number of other companies, in addition to running its own site. You will be using part of LookSmart when you choose AltaVista or Excite, for instance. Equally if you use MSN you'll be using LookSmart; major companies like BT, for example, also use Look-Smart technology. Consequently, getting indexed by LookSmart is a significant advantage. However, you can only be listed free of charge if you are a non-commercial site. You can find out more at its main home page:

http://www.looksmart.com

Applying to the top search engines...............................

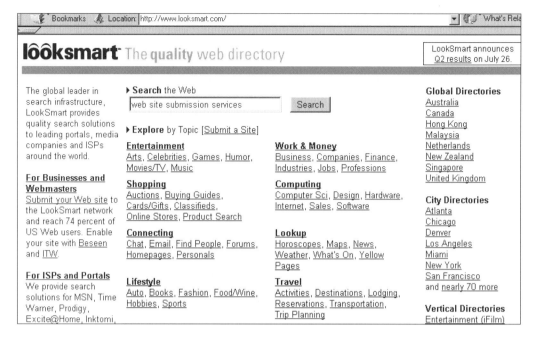

Fig. 24. LookSmart is a fast search engine that can also provide customised search facilities for your own web site.

Lycos

Lycos is one of the top search engines, powered by the same software that runs HotBot. Lycos appears to be aimed more at 'home' users – fine if this is a particular target for your web site. However, if you are aiming at business users, other search engines may produce more hits for you. That said, you should add your site to Lycos anyway since search engines are often a matter of personal choice. You can find two people in the same business using different search engines, so don't let the 'home user' appeal of Lycos put you off. Many people in business use this search engine every day.

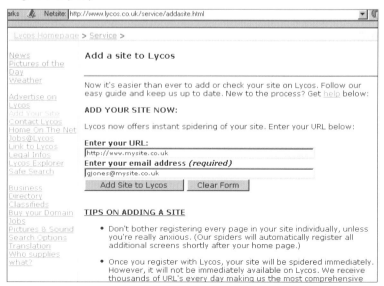

Fig. 25. Lycos provides a search engine accompanied by a range of features that viewers may find useful.

Applying to the top search engines

You can reach the Lycos submission page by going to its main UK home page:

http://www.lycos.co.uk

Then, scroll all the way down to the bottom of the screen, where in small type you will see Add your site to Lycos. Click on this link and you will be presented with a form to complete and some advice on getting your site listed. You will also be told on this page how long it will take to get your site listed. Be prepared for a long wait. Like most search engines, Lycos has a huge number of applications to process each day.

MSN

MSN (Microsoft Network) is used by many web surfers because you can set up a completely personalised 'home page' which appears each time you log on to the internet. In this way you can have a screen full of national news, your own favourite items, local weather and so on. Its main home page is at:

http://www.msn.com

MSN also incorporates a search engine that utilises LookSmart technology. However, you get the chance to search the web according to a number of different methods – using Excite, with MSN or via UKPlus, a specific directory of UK web sites (see Chapter 4).

To add your web site to MSN, you do not go to the main site at all. Instead you need to go to:

http://search.msn.co.uk/addurl.asp

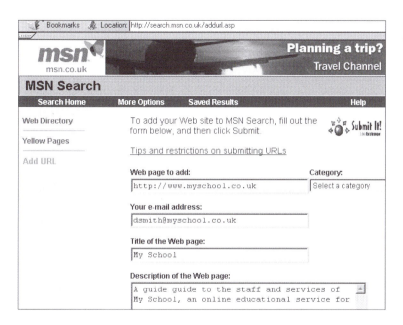

Fig. 26. Add your site to MSN at this page.

Applying to the top search engines

Complete the simple form and make sure you choose an appropriate category for your site. You may be rejected if you select the wrong category. Also, check the hints and tips section before you submit your page.

Scrub The Web

Scrub The Web is an unusual name for an unusual search engine. Its main home page is at:

> http://www.scrubtheweb.com

Set up by a web design company, Scrub The Web has affiliations to AltaVista, HotBot and InfoSeek. It works like this:

1. Someone searches for an item at Scrub The Web.
2. They receive a list of possible links.
3. At the bottom of the window is the option to find what they are looking for using other search engines (AltaVista, HotBot, InfoSeek).
4. The user clicks on one of these search engine links, and is presented with another list of possible sites.

The trick here is that the sites presented by the other search engines are filtered so that only those with links back to Scrub The Web are listed. This means that all you need to do is add a link to Scrub The Web to your web site and you will get priority listing in AltaVista, HotBot and InfoSeek, when they are searched through the Scrub The Web page. Another advantage of Scrub The Web is that your site will be automatically added to the index shortly after you submit it. There is no human intervention to analyse sites or to check they are editorially suitable (as is the case with most other search engines). This means you can gain rapid listing. To gain entry to Scrub The Web go to:

> http://www.scrubtheweb.com/addurl.html

To ensure that you gain the maximum from the tie-up with the other search engines click on Get Scrubbed which is at the bottom of the submission page.

Snap

Snap is a search engine run by the media conglomerate NBC. The site is heavily biased towards the USA, with its 'local' service covering the 50 states of the union and not beyond! This quibble aside, Snap is a fast, easy to use service that is fast becoming a significant competitor to the older, more established companies like Yahoo!. Its main home page is at:

> http://www.snap.com

Snap is a very fast service that returns searches much faster than the

Applying to the top search engines

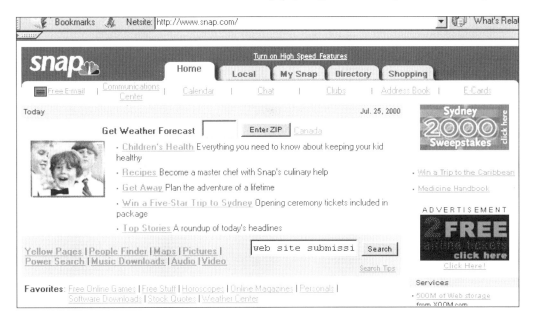

Fig. 27. Snap is a breeze to use, but very complex to get listed with.

competition, hence its increasing popularity. The rapidity of its service is not matched by the speed with which you can submit your site, though!

First you need to visit the home page as shown above. Then select List your Site, at the bottom of the screen. This takes you to another page where you have to select Submit your Site. You are then transported to yet another page, where you must select a topic area under which you want listing. You may need to click through several pages until you find the category you want to be listed under. Having done this, you then need to register as a Snap Member, which takes a few minutes. Finally, you will arrive at a submission page, which will ask you for a considerable amount of information.

Snap is a great service and one that you should be listed on, but be prepared for a frustrating submission process. Not even Yahoo!'s submission procedure, which many people criticise, is as complex as this.

WebCrawler

WebCrawler is a clean and uncluttered search engine that provides fast and easy searches. It is popular because it is not 'fussed' with a host of add-on features which may be tempting but which get in the way of the primary task of searching. Its main home page is at:

http://www.webcrawler.com

Like many other search engines, WebCrawler is not completely independent – it is owned by Excite. However, you need to submit to WebCrawler separately. To do this go to:

http://www.webcrawler.com/info/add_url/

Here you fill in a simple form and your web site will be indexed.

Applying to the top search engines..

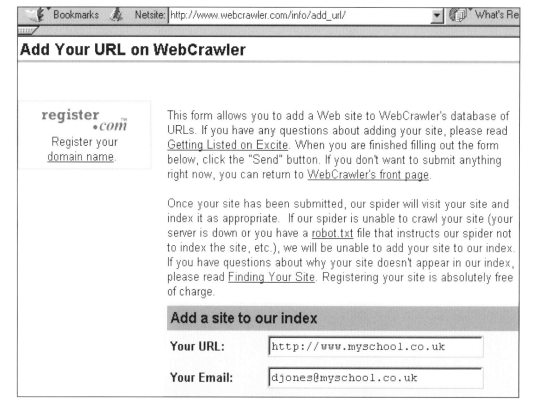

Fig. 28. WebCrawler is a straightforward search engine that is clean and uncluttered. That's why many people like it so much.

Yahoo!

If you do not add your web site to any other search engine, you simply must add it to Yahoo!, because roughly half of all web searches in the world are conducted at Yahoo!, despite the fact that there are thousands of other ways in which searches can be performed. If you are not listed by Yahoo!, you will not be visible to most web surfers. Yahoo!'s main home page is at:

http://www.yahoo.com

The Yahoo! submission system requires you to select a category before you make your application. This means you need to trawl through Yahoo! to identify a suitable part of its database in which you want to be listed. Since Yahoo! is vast, this can be rather time-consuming, but it is definitely worthwhile. If you submit to Yahoo! for an unsuitable category, you will not get listed. Real live editors – who process all applications – will decide whether or not to include your site. Selecting the part of Yahoo! in which you want to be included is a necessary task – do not neglect it.

To submit your site to Yahoo! all you need do is search for similar sites. You can then find which categories they are listed in. Once you are in that category, scroll to the bottom of the screen and click on Suggest a Site.

.... **Applying to the top search engines**

This brings up a page of instructions and a button labelled Proceed to Step One. You are then stepped through a series of pages until you can finally submit your site. If your web site could be included in multiple categories, you can mention these when you make your submission. This means you need to have researched all the possible categories before you start your submission process.

Once your site has been submitted, be prepared for a long wait before it appears. Yahoo! receives thousands of applications each day, and all of them are processed by human beings, not by computer robots. This means it may take several weeks – even a couple of months – before your web site appears on the Yahoo! search system.

▶ *Tip* – Do not be tempted to submit your site if you have the address but haven't yet started to build it. Some people do this in the hope that Yahoo! will list their site by the time they have finished constructing the pages. This will not happen, since all incomplete sites are rejected straight away.

If your site is accepted by Yahoo! you will receive an email confirming this. If you don't get an email within six weeks, the chances are your site has been rejected. This means you have either not selected the right category, or your site is deemed unsuitable. To correct this, fine-tune your site and re-select your category before making another submission.

One of the main reasons for rejection by Yahoo! is that sites are not focused on a particular topic. If your web site is trying to be all things to all people, it will probably be rejected by Yahoo!.

One final tip about Yahoo! – it doesn't use meta tags, which shows that even though meta tags are important, they are not vital to success!

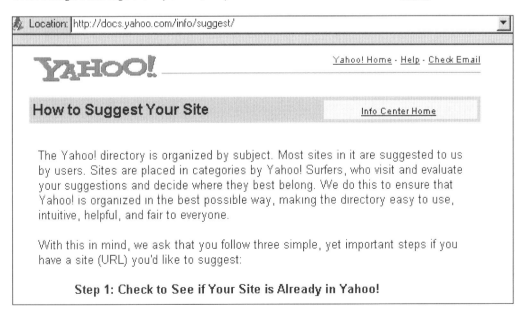

Fig. 29. Suggest a site to Yahoo! and it will be checked by human beings before it is added. This process can take several weeks.

4 Getting listed throughout the web

In this chapter we will explore:

▶ *internet directories*
▶ *'what's new' lists*
▶ *award schemes*
▶ *web rings*
▶ *reciprocal links*
▶ *Usenet messages*
▶ *increasing your hit rate*

There are many different ways in which you can get your site listed, outside of search engines. These include internet directories, 'what's new' lists, various award schemes, web rings, reciprocal links, and Usenet messages.

Getting listed in internet directories

Directories are specialist web sites that list other web sites – it's as simple as that. They are almost as popular as search engines, and so are an important promotional resource. Sometimes they are called guides, or reviews. The difference between a directory of this nature and a search engine is straightforward.

Directory services do not maintain complex indexes allowing you to search for keywords. Instead the directories and guides list sites according to pre-determined categories. Many of the search engines, such as Yahoo! and Lycos, include directories as well as keyword location capabilities. However, the pure directories do not index your sites with crawlers or spiders and therefore provide more limited search capabilities for users.

The advantage of a directory is that a web surfer can go to a specified category and see a complete list of possible sites that may be of use. With search engines, finding the same list may take a number of different attempts using various keywords.

Finding out about general directories
To submit your site to a directory, you first need to find a list of directories! There are two ways to do this. Firstly, you can use a large directory-based search engine such as Yahoo! to find you a list of directories. You can find a list of several hundred at:

http://dir.yahoo.com/Computers_and_Internet/Internet/World_Wide_Web/Searching_the_Web/Web_Directories/

You should also try:

http://uk.dir.yahoo.com/Computers_and_Internet/Internet/World_Wide_Web/Searching_the_Web/Web_Directories/

Getting listed throughout the web

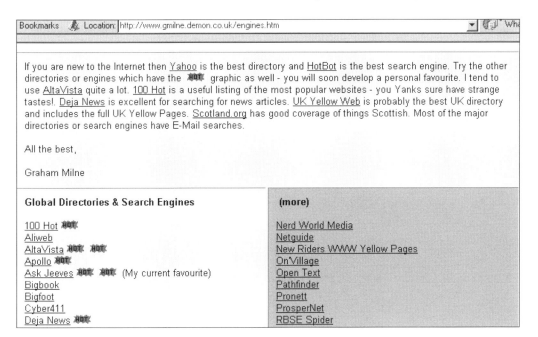

Alternatively you can try some of the web sites that act as directories of directories. One is '1 Dir of 1 Dirs' and can be found at:

http://www.gmilne.demon.co.uk/engines.htm

Fig. 30.1 Dir of 1 Dirs is the strange name given to this useful directory of directories.

Aleph Search
http://www.albedo.co.uk/sites/aleph/
Another useful site of directories is Aleph Search.

Fig. 31. Aleph Search is an excellent directory of directories to help you start your submission process.

Getting listed throughout the web ....

Fig. 32. AllSearch Engines has categories of search engines and directories for you to check.

AllSearch Engines
http://www.allsearchengines.co.uk/
One of the most useful sites is AllSearch Engines. This lists and categorises search engines and directories.

When you visit any of these sites, or look at the lists at Yahoo!, you will discover that there are hundreds of general web directories to which you can add your site. In addition, many of the lists you will have already generated only cover 'general' directories. We have yet to discover the thousands of subject specific directories!

Finding out about specific directories
Your web site should be aimed at a specific set of viewers, which will have its own directory. You need to be added to that target audience's directory, since many people use subject-specific directories to find what they are looking for. This is because many subject directories are better at categorising items than general lists, simply because they know the field better. This means it is often easier to find what you want at a specific subject directory than a general listing.

▶ *Example* – Imagine you worked in the training industry. You would probably find what you are looking for in your particular world much more quickly at Training Pages (http://www.trainingpages.co.uk/), a directory of British training resources, than using a search engine.

Specific industries
To find directories in your specific industry go to:

http://dir.yahoo.com/Business_and_Economy/Directories/Companies/

Getting listed throughout the web

Finding a local directory
To find a local directory go to:

> http://dir.yahoo.com/Regional/Countries/United_Kingdom/
> Computers_and_Internet/Internet/World_Wide_Web/Searching_
> the_Web/Web_Directories/

Finding specific search engines
You can also find specific search engines at AllSearch Engines:

> http://www.allsearchengines.co.uk

Another site you might like to try is the Search Engine Colossus that lists directories under various categories:

> http://www.searchenginecolossus.com/

Choosing a directory
Some people believe that you should enter your web site name into as many directories as possible. Others take the view that you should be selective to make sure you achieve quality links. The reasoning is that you will waste time entering your details into a directory that might not lead to many hits. Alternatively, the 'enter everything' lobby points out that the more links you have around the world wide web, the higher your ranking in some of the more important search directories. Hence, the argument goes, you can gain by entering your web site in every directory, no matter how small or obscure.

Both sides of this debate have some merit, but if you enter your name into every directory you will waste a considerable amount of time, since

Fig. 33. Searchability has useful reviews of search engines and directories.

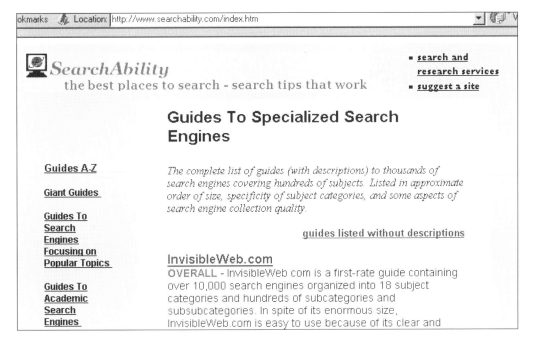

55

Getting listed throughout the web

there are several thousand of them. You therefore do need to be selective if you are to make the best use of your time.

To help make your selection you may find Searchability helpful. This is a review site that rates search engines and directories and has handy reviews of each. These reviews will be useful in helping you make your selection of places to which you could submit your web site. You can find Searchability at:

http://www.searchability.com/index.htm

The principles of selection
Select a directory using the following criteria:

1. Does the site look professional?

2. Does the site work properly? (Check a few links to see.)

3. Is there an email address or are contact details available?

4. What other sites are listed and are they the kind you would like to be associated with?

5. Can you find your way around the site easily? If you can't the chances are other people would find it difficult to locate your link.

6. Is the site run by a business or does it seem as though an internet hobbyist puts it together? (A hobbyist is less likely to update the directory on a regular basis.)

Submitting your site to directories
Once you have made a selection of directories you will need to submit your details. There are as many ways of doing this, as there are directories. Each has a different online form to complete and varied information they require from you. You will need to set aside some time (remembering you will be connected throughout) to complete the submissions.

Most directories will have a Submit Your Site button or an Add URL link. You can go direct to the relevant pages from AllSearch Engines, which has a Submit button against the names of various directory services it lists. Go to:

http://www.allsearchengines.co.uk

Submitting automatically to directories
As with search engines, there are various services you can buy that will complete the tedious task of submission on your behalf. Most of the programs and the web services mentioned in Chapter 2 can do this for you – the main exception being Web Position Gold, which does not include directories amongst its possibilities, instead sticking to the Top 13 search engines. One of the better directory submission programs is Traffic Builder:

http://www.intelliquis.com/products/traffic.stm

······························· **Getting listed throughout the web**

The Microsoft Submit It web-based service is also very powerful for directory submissions. You can find out more at:

http://submitit.bcentral.com/

If you intend submitting to many directories, or if you simply can't be bothered to perform a proper analysis of the ones available, then you should use some kind of automatic submission.

Directories you should not miss
No matter how good your search for directories or how valuable the automatic submission services may be, there are some directories you should not miss and which you should make every attempt to enter manually. These include:

1. Scoot
2. The Open Directory Project
3. UK Plus
4. Yellow Pages

Scoot
http://www.scoot.co.uk
Scoot is a web directory of British businesses. If you run any kind of business in the UK, get yourself listed at Scoot. It has thousands of categories and anyone looking for a business in your category or area will find you. Scoot is particularly valuable if you provide a local service, as the directory is broken down into regions. Adding your site is a simple and quick process. All you have to do is press the Submit button and follow the instructions.

Fig. 34. Scoot is an essential directory if you are running a business in the UK.

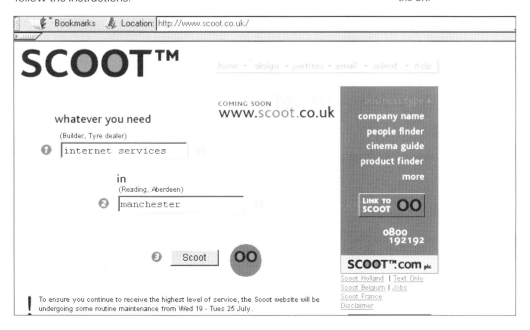

Getting listed throughout the web ....

The Open Directory Project
http://dmoz.org/
This is an enormous site of links providing a huge directory of web sites throughout the world. The difference between this directory and something like Yahoo! is that the company running this directory – Netscape – does not employ the editors who select the sites. Instead, there are thousands of editors around the world who look after specific sections of the directory. Anyone can volunteer to be an editor and look after a particular category. The idea is that with tens of thousands of people constructing the directory it will be more rapidly produced than with a handful of editors at a search engine. Volunteer editors need to show some degree of expertise in the category they wish to organise and they receive training on how to keep their little section of the directory up to date.

You can add your web site name to the Open Directory Project and one of the many editors will check out your site and add it to the listings. Sometimes this can be done within hours, as opposed to the weeks or even months of some search engines. One good reason for using the Open Directory Project is that the directory is used in searches made by Netscape, Lycos and HotBot. Another advantage of the Open Directory Project is that the editors frequently have a vested interest in keeping their category up to date and well organised. They are often running their own business and use the directory to promote their service, so these editors keep their sections well ordered and up to date.

To submit your web site name go to the page shown above. You will find an Add URL button on the top right of the page. However, click through the various categories and find one that you think you should be listed under. Scroll down to the bottom of the page and see if there is an editor's name and link. If not, there will be a This Category Needs an

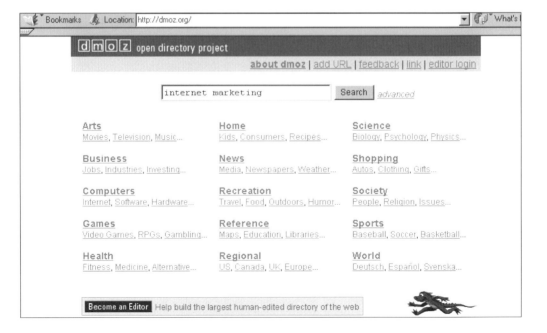

Fig. 35. The Open Directory Project is an amazing web directory and one that you will not want to miss.

Getting listed throughout the web

Editor note. All you have to do is click on the Become an Editor link and you can apply to edit that particular category. This may be of real value if you are trying to promote your service, so it is worth checking.

UK Plus
http://www.ukplus.co.uk
UK Plus is one of the main UK directories, listing only sites from the UK. It is run by the same company that produces *The Daily Mail*. It is one of the largest internet companies in the UK. It attracts lots of hits from families since it has a 'safe for families' searching capability. This brings up a list of links that have been verified as being suitable for all the family, filtering out undesirable sites from being shown. You can search the main part of UK Plus, but this merely uses the InfoSeek search engine. To make sure you are listed within the main part of UK Plus, ask for your site to be checked. To do this, click on Add a Site at the bottom of the home page.

Fig. 36. UK Plus is one of the major directories of web sites based in the UK, providing a local perspective compared with many of the American-biased search engines.

Yellow Pages
http://www.yellowpages.co.uk/Aboutus
If you run a business you can get a free entry into one of the many Yellow Pages products, including their web service Yell. To find out what kind of entry you can receive you need to make an application to Yellow Pages. They will then contact you to let you know the options available. This might seem cumbersome, but it is worthwhile remembering that Yellow Pages is still the first place many people turn to when trying to find a business. So getting a listing could dramatically improve your web site hit rate. The application form you need is available at the page shown above.

Get a 'what's new' listing

If your web site is new, make sure you submit it to a 'what's new' service.

Getting listed throughout the web ....

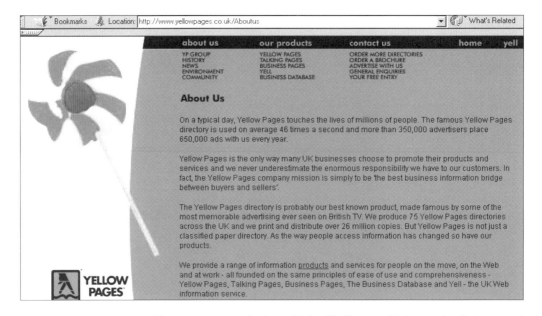

Fig. 37. Yellow Pages asks you to fill in this form to find out more about the free listings you can receive.

Fig. 38. Get a listing in What's Nu if you want to promote a new web site.

There are some web sites which will offer to publish your details in general and categorised lists. People often check these services to find out the latest in a particular field. You should make sure you get your new web site listed. To do this, go to the following sites:

http://www.whatsnu.com/

http://www.nerdworld.com/nwadd.html

Getting listed throughout the web

Applying for an award

Throughout the internet there are all kinds of award schemes that could be useful in promoting your web site. You can win an award for your web site's design or for the way your site is run, plus there are many other kinds of prizes on offer. The main prize you are looking for, however, is the ability to have a link to your site on one of the award directories. This will drive more traffic your way and will also help improve your ranking in some of the search engines.

There are various award sites including 'sites of the day' and 'sites of the week'. There are also various annual awards, even awards of 'the hour'. You will even find awards for the most useless web site. You name it, there's probably an award somewhere for it on the world wide web. Submitting your URL for an award can generate extra traffic and help promote your web site. There are several hundred different award schemes and sites. Hence you might like to search for awards that apply to your particular sector.

Advertising, Marketing and Promotional Services
http://www.amps-inc.com/awards.html
A good place to start looking is Advertising, Marketing and Promotional Services Inc. Here you will find a list of a host of award schemes as well as information on how to apply. Should you win an award, be sure to publicise your success to help generate even more hits for your site.

Fig. 39. This handy directory of web site award schemes is a good place to start to make sure your site gets recognition.

Joining a web ring

A web ring is a way of increasing traffic to your site as a result of sharing links with similar web sites. Each member site of the web ring carries links to a handful of other members. In this way an extensive array of links to similar sites can be established.

Getting listed throughout the web ....

There are many different kinds of web rings with a variety of arrangements as to how they are organised and the commitment you must make. Usually, though, you have to enter your site for approval. Once this has occurred you have to add a link to the web ring to ensure you get links from other members. Often you will be given some code that needs adding to your site. This code (in HTML or as a JavaScript) will place a series of links to a handful of other sites involved in the web ring. These sites are randomly allocated and your pages will have different links each time they are loaded. In return, other members of the web ring will feature links to your site on a random basis.

Advantages of joining a web ring
The result of a web ring is that your web site's address appears from time to time on other web sites that are related to your particular topic. This increases the chance of someone wishing to jump to your site, since they are already reading material that is your subject area and hence should be interested. Another advantage is the more links you have on your site and the more incoming links there are to your pages, the greater your chances of success in being listed by the search engines.

Disadvantages of joining a web ring
The downside of web rings is that they can lead your viewers away to the competition! Equally, you have no control to the links that appear on your site and you may not always approve of the kind of web site that your site recommends! Other web rings do not require you to have links. Instead you join a directory of other web sites which all have similar topics as yours.

Finding a web ring
There are over 80,000 web rings on the internet, so you should be selective. Look for a web ring that has plenty of links and one that appears

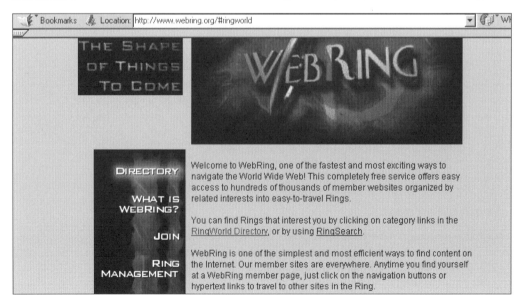

Fig. 40. WebRing provides a complete directory of all the various individual web rings that exist.

Getting listed throughout the web

professional. Anything that looks like it has been produced by an internet hobbyist should be avoided as it could harm the reputation of your professional site. You can find a list of all the various web rings at the WebRing Directory:

http://www.webring.org/#ringworld

Adding reciprocal links to your site

One good way of generating more traffic and improving your search-engine ranking is to place reciprocal links on your site. Essentially this is rather like having your own web ring. Unlike a web ring you get to decide who joins and dictate the terms under which they'll display your site. All you need do to gain reciprocal links is to invite people who you think would link to your site to consider doing so. These are some of the people you could invite:

1. friends
2. family
3. colleagues
4. suppliers
5. customers
6. your web designer
7. your ISP

Just ask them if they would carry a link to your site on one of their web pages. In return, offer to have a link to their site on yours. Explain the benefit of doing this. Point out that it will help to promote each other's site as well as help to boost search engine rankings for both of you. To help your potential collaborator, you could even provide them with the code they might like to insert to ensure they can easily add the link. The code you could send them would look something like this:

<A HREF="http://www.yourdomainname.com/">YOUR LINK HEADING</A> Some text here to provide a summary of your site.

Using banner links
You might even want to provide a graphic link or a banner. To create your own banner you can find ideas and support at Banner Warehouse:

http://www.stuff.uk.com/banners/index.shtml

You can also get a banner made from the elements on your existing web site using an online design service. A fast service can be found at:

http://gwwebdesign.com

You just give them your web site address and they will design a banner within a couple of days for $75.

Whatever you can do to make it easy for someone to link to your site, so much the better. You can also get reciprocal links from people you don't

Getting listed throughout the web

Fig. 41. If you want to have mutual exchanges of links you can find out more at Reciprocal Links.

even know! There are some schemes on the internet that allow you to get links to your site placed on another web site, providing you link to the other site. A good place to start is Reciprocal Links.

Reciprocal Links
http://www.reciprocallink.com/
This web site includes a directory of organisations that are prepared to have a link to your site, providing you carry their designated link as well.

Some web sites will even allow you to add your web site address to their links page using a form. However, it is usually courteous to offer these sites the same possibility at yours. This means you may need to add a links page that allows such a 'free for all' listing. If you do this, you will need to monitor the page closely as you may end up with links on your web site that you do not want! You can add a 'free for all' page using a script that you can get from Matt's Script Archive at:

http://www.worldwidemart.com/scripts/links.shtml

You should also consider adding your site to the various free for all services that are on offer. The web site submission program, Traffic Builder, includes a lot of free for all sites in its listing. Exploit Submission Wizard will also send your site to free for all links pages. You can also find plenty of other free for all sites by using your favourite search engine to look for 'free for all'.

Using Usenet to promote your site

There are thousands of newsgroups on Usenet, around 80,000 in all. This is a large and old-established part of the internet that is like a huge bulletin board, where literally millions of messages are posted. Each newsgroup is dedicated to a particular topic, so there is bound to be at least one that

Getting listed throughout the web

should be useful in promoting your web site. All you have to do is post a message announcing your site, to the newsgroups relevant to your particular field.

Finding newsgroups

▶ *Microsoft Internet Explorer* – If you use this browser you can access the newsgroups by using the Read News command from the Mail and News sub-menu of the Tools menu.

▶ *Netscape* – If you use this browser you can gain access to Usenet by choosing Newsgroups from the Communicator menu.

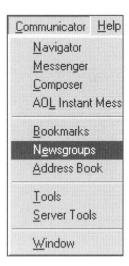

In either case you can then search for newsgroups that are related to your field of interest. Most newsgroups include a keyword in their title such as:

uk.sport.football.clubs.Bradford-city

The first word in the newsgroup address indicates the kind of material that is contained inside. Clearly, 'uk' indicates that it is a newsgroup relating to UK material. There are numerous other country codes, such as 'it' for Italy and 'fr' for France. There are also several global newsgroups which have different top-level categories. These include:

Top level category	Subject matter
alt	alternative material – a free-for-all area
comp	computers
Microsoft	anything to do with Microsoft
misc	miscellaneous subjects
news	news
rec	recreation (such as sports, hobbies, pastimes)
sci	science (including a sub-category Med for medicine)
soc	social topics and sociology
talk	chat and discussions

Whenever you launch a web site, or substantially change it, send a message to the relevant newsgroups and you will increase your hit rate. Many people follow newsgroups, and announcing new web sites is a common practice. Before sending a message, spend some time reading messages in the newsgroup to get a sense of what would be acceptable.

▶ *Tip* – Make sure that your message includes the full address of the web site (including http://). People reading your message will then simply be able to click onto the address and open up your page right away. This saves them the bother of having to type it in, thus improving your chances of success.

65

Getting listed throughout the web ....

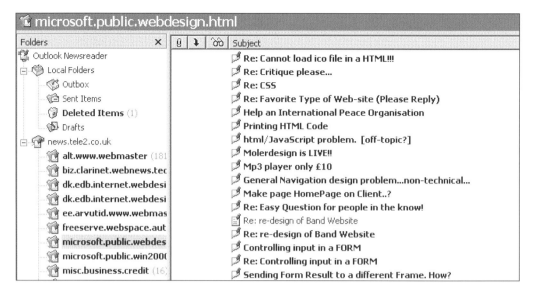

Fig. 42. Use newsgroups to announce your site and you could further increase the number of hits you receive.

Increasing your hit rate

The more links there are to your site around the internet, the more successful you will be. No matter how good your listing in search engines, only about half of all hits come from them. Many people rely on recommended sites in directories, and on links from other web pages. The more links you can create elsewhere on the web, the better.

In addition, the more links there are to your web site, the greater its chances of being ranked high by the search engines. Your time spent in arranging all these extra links will pay off handsomely. Some large web sites have people whose sole job is to encourage other sites to link to them. Even if you only have a small web site, you should adopt this kind of attitude. The big sites have become big because there are millions of links to them. Make sure your site has plenty of links, and you too could benefit.

This table shows the total number of hits for the site, how many were successful, how many failed, and calculates the percentage of hits that failed. It may help you in determining the reliability of your site.

Technical Statistics and Analysis	
Total Hits	117418
Successful Hits	114502
Failed Hits	2916
Failed Hits as Percent	2.48%
Cached Hits	20422
Cached Hits as Percent	17.39%

5 More free online promotion

In this chapter we will explore:

▶ *press releases*
▶ *targeted email*
▶ *don't fall foul of the data laws*
▶ *banner exchanges*
▶ *maximising your free publicit*

Although listing your site on search engines and in directories is very useful, you are relying on people searching for your keywords. Depending on how specialist your site is, you might be in for a long wait. That's why it is necessary to promote your site in other ways to make sure that people really do hear about your web site. There are three principal ways you can do this for free on the internet. These are:

1. press releases
2. targeted email
3. banner exchanges

Creating online press releases

There are some free press-release distribution services that you can use to announce your site. These services will make your press release available to journalists who may then use your material in newspapers, magazines or online. However, a press release is almost certain to be thrown away or ignored if it is mere 'puffery'. Journalists need a story; simply telling them you have a new site is not news. So, to announce your site you need to create something newsworthy.

Popular stories are based around themes such as:

(a) celebrities

(b) surveys

(c) statistics

If you can get a celebrity to be your first registered user, for instance, you have a story. If you can conduct a survey about your specialist field and announce the results on your site, you have a story. Or, if you can find out some relevant statistics and publish them on your site, you also have a story. Having a new web site is not news – after all there are tens of thousand of them launched every day. News is 'new' – something people did not know beforehand. We all know web sites are launched every minute so it is not news. Your press release needs to provide something that is novel or unusual for a journalist to be interested in using the material.

More free online promotion

Fig. 43. Press release writing tips can help you ensure your PR materials gain wide coverage.

Web sites to help you with press releases

To find out more about writing press releases you could explore the following sites:

http://www.press-release-writing.com/10_essential_tips.htm

http://www.hgmarketing.com/articles/freepub2.shtml

http://www.greatpromote.com/guide/stucker.html

You could also refer to the paperback *Writing a Press Release* by Peter Bartram, published by HowTo Books (ISBN: 1 857 03485 6).

All these resources tell you one key fact: keep your press release short. If it is more than 150 words it is too long. If the press release has done its job, a journalist will contact you for more information. Tell them the bare bones of the story, and whet their appetite. Don't try to tell the whole story. If you want to learn more about press-release writing there are various courses you can go on as well. You could try the following company for advice:

http://www.mediafirst.co.uk

Submitting your press release online

Once you have written your press release you should submit it to those journalists who might find it interesting. A number of different services maintain such mailing lists of reporters and many of them are free. You will need to check that the services you choose actually reach your target audience of journalists.

....**More free online promotion**

1. If the company distributes to computer journalists and your press release is about your new web site on horse racing, you are unlikely to get much coverage.

2. You should also make sure that the list is an opt-in list. In other words, the journalists have asked to receive material from this service. Otherwise your press release may be seen as an irritant and could be ignored.

Some press-release services do not send out their clients' press releases, but make them available in an online directory instead. If that is the case, find out as much information as you can, including details of how much traffic the site receives. Submitting a press release to a service that journalists rarely use will not do you much good. Some press release directory sites attract plenty of journalistic interest, others do not.

Finally, before submitting your releases, make sure that you check the detailed instructions. Some services ask you to fill in an on-screen form, others ask you to send an email with a plain text attachment. Some ask you to submit material in other formats. Be sure to follow the directions you are given, otherwise your press release may not be used. The time spent in preparing the different formats will help your chances of success and therefore provide even more hits to your web site.

Make sure that you include your web site address using the 'http://' at the beginning. This will mean that people can click on the address and go straight to your site without having to type it in. Having this hyperlink in your press release will help journalists who receive it by email. It will also boost traffic to your site if your text is posted on the directory of the service you use, since there will be an extra link to your site on the internet, helping to raise your search engine status.

Choosing a press release service
There are several hundred free press-release distribution services around. You could spend many happy hours going through them all! To find a service that specialises in your topic, carry out an advanced search using your favourite search engine. Simply make a search for:

"free press release distribution" + "your topic"

This will limit the list of distribution services you could use. All you need do is check out each web site you find and work out which one is most likely to help you reach your target audience.

Most online press-release services, however, offer widespread distribution to a whole host of journalists. Even so, they can limit the spread of your material to particular categories of writers. If you find a service that makes press releases available without any kind of targeting, forget it. You will be wasting your time, because untargeted releases almost always get ignored.

Some of the most free popular press release distribution services include PR Web and The Web Wire.

More free online promotion

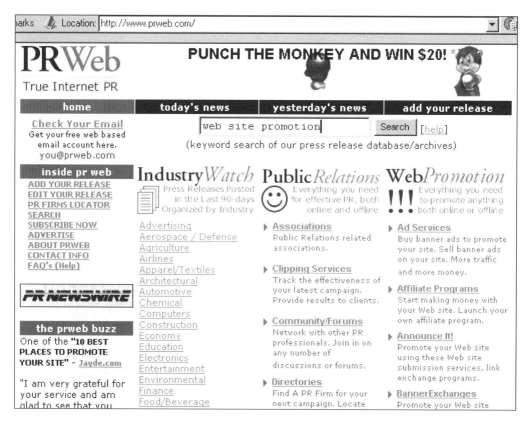

Fig. 44. Submit your press release via PR Web and you'll get maximum exposure.

PR Web
http://www.prweb.com
PR Web is a highly professional site that provides a host of services and links to public relations material. The site does not distribute your release, but makes it available on its site — a sort of huge bulletin board of press releases. The site is sorted by category, and journalists can visit their own particular field of interest and check out the latest news. PR Web also has a link to a paid-for distribution service at which you can claim a discount.

The Web Wire
http://www.webwire.com
The Web Wire provides a centralised news service to which you can add your press release. You can also choose from extra options, such as adding your headline to a scrolling list of the 'latest news'. In addition, The Web Wire has links to paid for services that will assess your press release and suggest further cost-based distribution.

Using targeted email to promote your web site

The press release distribution services are little more than targeted email lists, specifically aiming at journalists. You could use this concept to deliver email messages to potential viewers of your web site, announcing it directly to the people you want to reach.

Email addresses are everywhere and you can collect them from all

More free online promotion

sorts of places. However, there are two things that can prevent you from using them!

▶ data protection legislation

▶ anti-spamming policies

Don't fall foul of the data laws
The Data Protection Commissioner in the UK is responsible for ensuring that any data people hold is only used for legitimate purposes and is not collected unlawfully. The various Data Protection Acts are extremely complex. Even simple things could lead to an unwitting breach of the legislation.

In essence, if you have on your computer anyone's personal details, such as an address in a letter, you need to register with the Data Protection Commissioner.

Retaining any data whatsoever about other people on your computer requires registration. If you do not register, and you keep personal information about other people on your computer, you have already broken UK law! Even if you keep the details on paper, rather than on the computer, you need to register. Hence, if you were to collect some email addresses and did not register with the Data Protection Commissioner, your legal position begins to get shaky! To check the situation and apply for registration if you need it, go to:

The Data Protection Registrar
http://www.dataprotection.gov.uk/dprhome.htm
You can also use a document from the Data Protection Commissioner

Fig. 45. Make sure you are registered with the UK Data Protection Commissioner if you wish to store data about potential viewers of your site.

More free online promotion

which asks you a series of questions to determine whether or not you need to register. This is at:

http://www.dpr.gov.uk/tnrsa.doc

If you do need to register, you will find that you are required to undertake certain actions, particularly in maintaining security of the data you record.

Beware of spamming
Spamming means sending out large numbers of unsolicited emails. It is considered worse than direct mail because it is so pervasive. With direct mail, considerable amounts of money need to be spent. Even though you may well dislike the handful of unsolicited letters you get each week, you should be grateful the cost of direct mail is so high. Otherwise you could be overwhelmed by it. Direct email costs next to nothing, so you can receive vast amounts of unsolicited, boring, trivial, or downright disgusting messages. If you are a regular internet user, receiving hundreds of unsolicited emails every day is quite possible. You can see why it is so disliked. You can find out more about spamming at the Coalition Against Unsolicited Commercial Email.

Fig. 46. Don't let your email get caught up in the spamming debate. Send out emails wisely to promote your site; otherwise you will find yourself on the receiving end of some negative feedback.

Coalition Against Unsolicited Commercial Email
http://www.cauce.org/
Run by volunteers, this site is designed to provide information about the problems of junk email, some proposed solutions, and to provide resources for the net community to make informed choices about the issues surrounding junk email.

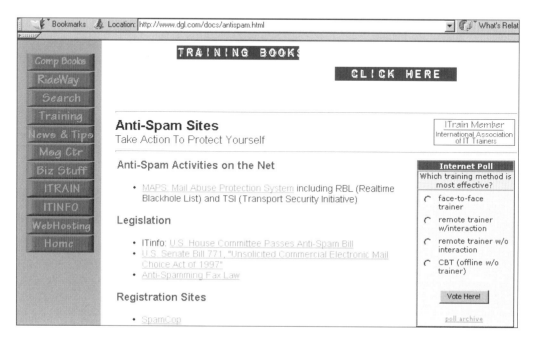

More free online promotion

There are dozens of other web sites devoted to spamming and to halting abuse of email. You can find a directory of useful resources at:

http://www.dgl.com/docs/antispam.html

You do not want to become listed as someone who sends out spams. You want a positive status for your internet activities, not a rapidly spreading reputation of being a spammer. So if you want to use emails to promote your site, do so without spamming.

Email people who 'opt in' to your kind of message
The best way to promote your site via email is to send messages only to those people who have said they want them. This is called an 'opt in' method of sending emails, since the recipients have said they are happy to have them. Happily, there are plenty of opt-in mailing services which you can use to send out an announcement of your new web site. Sadly, they all charge a fee, but there is a way of generating your own opt-in email list.

Establishing your own mailing list
You will need to generate your own mailing list to send out announcements about your web site. An excellent way of doing this is to use the ListBot service of Microsoft Bcentral. You can find more details at:

ListBot
http://www.listbot.com/
Two kinds of service are available, one is free and one costs $99 a year. The free service provides almost everything you need; you will only need the paid for service if you want to collect extra data about your mailing list

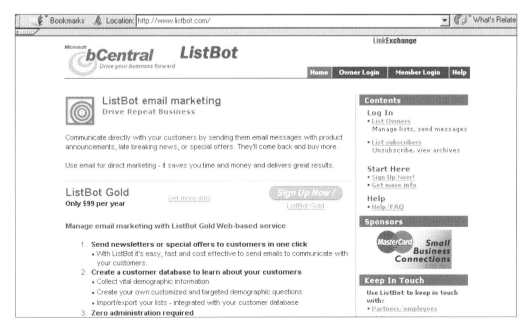

Fig. 47. Use the ListBot free service, and you will be able to set up and manage your own mailing list.

More free online promotion

subscribers. In either event, you can set up an opt-in mailing service. You simply add the link to your web site and run the service from ListBot. You can then email a large list of people automatically. You can also add your ListBot invitation to an email message.

When you announce your web site, via press releases and so on, include your ListBot details. People will be able to opt in to your own mailing list in this way. You can also send the ListBot details to your existing contacts or even via direct mail. This will encourage even more people to sign up. Before long you will have your own mailing list to which you can send regular announcements about your web site.

Consider an email newsletter or ezine

One of the promotional techniques you can use with an email list is to send a regular newsletter or ezine (electronic magazine). This is cheaper than a traditional newsletter and is targeted at people who really want to hear from you – those who have opted into your service. New research shows that targeted email newsletters are by far the best way of attracting people.[2] They score an amazing 63 per cent response rate – pretty stunning compared with the average 3 per cent response to standard direct mail.

Your email newsletter can contain tips and advice relating to your subject, as well as updates about your web site and any advertisements you wish to carry.

The Ezine Factory

http://www.ezinefactory.co.za/infopages/ezines.htm

You can find out more about creating and using email newsletters here. A useful feature of the page is its long list of links to other help web sites on this topic.

Fig. 48. Check out the E-zine Factory for advice on how to create your own email newsletters.

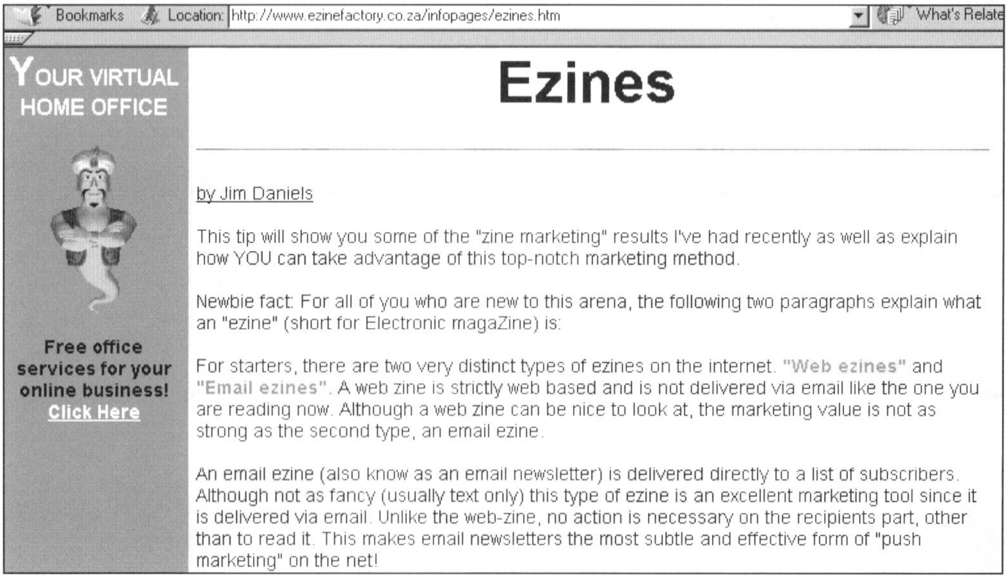

2. See http://resources.hitbox.com/cgi-bin/page.cgi?promoting/king

More free online promotion

Be seen with banners

Banners are the colourful strips of advertising material that you see at the top of many web pages. They have some value as a promotional tool, but this is limited. When banners were first introduced in the late 1990s they were a novelty, and triggered a great response. They have since become old hat, and fewer than 5 per cent of viewers click on them.

However, do not let this put you off. Banner advertising is much more important than the statistics would have us believe.

▶ *Tip* – If your banner is a regular feature on the internet, you create awareness, even if you do not achieve 'click through' (people clicking on your banner to reach your site).

Much advertising does not lead to direct action. Instead, it provides a positive reinforcement about a product or company. Advertisers know that their advertisements rarely result in immediate sales, but they are important in creating a positive psychological environment in which sales can take place.

For instance, have you ever rushed out and bought a Coca Cola simply because you saw a TV advert with happy people singing on it? Most unlikely. But did the happy singing advert put the words 'Coca Cola' back into your mind again? Almost certainly. Advertising is much more about reminding and reinforcing than about straight selling.

You will see much criticism about banner advertising on the internet. That's because people are analysing the effect of banners on click-through rates. What they should be measuring is the impact of banners on reminding and reinforcing. This will be much more powerful. Banner advertising does have its place in promoting your site, though the impact will not be as noticeable as having a high search engine ranking. Even so, you should consider having a banner for your web site.

Get free banner placements
Although banners are advertisements, there is a way to get yours published free of charge. This is using a banner exchange system. The idea is that you sign up for an exchange scheme, and submit your banner advertisement to the scheme; you then place an advertising 'holder' on your web site for a reciprocal advert. When your web page is opened by one of your viewers, an advert is called up from the exchange system. This records a hit at your site and ensures you get an advert in return. The more hits you get, the more reciprocal advertisements you get at other sites.

Used effectively, banner exchange systems can lead to many extra surfers finding their way to your site. You can find out more about banner advertising at:

http://www.eboz.com/advice/banner_advertising/

Using banner exchanges
There are hundreds of banner exchanges available, which vary in the kind of service they provide. For example:

Articles
- E-Commerce
- Internet Marketing
- Miscellaneous
- Top CEO Interview
- Web Site Design
- Success

Quick Tips
- Internet Marketing
- Internet Statistics
- Internet Terms
- Paint Shop Pro
- Photoshop
- Programming
- Web Site Design

More free online promotion

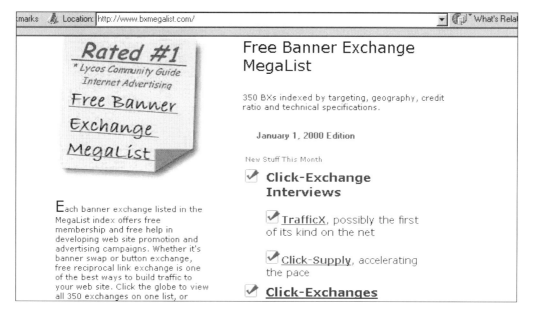

Fig. 49. Find a banner exchange service at BX Exchange and your advertisement could soon be seen in many places around the world wide web.

1. There is a banner exchange service called Sex Swap, which provides advertising exchanges for adult sites.

2. There is an exchange known as Kentish Exchange for web sites based in the Garden of England.

3. The ZineX exchange is purely intended for literary web sites.

You can find a full list of more than 350 banner exchanges at:

http://www.bxmegalist.com/

There are some well-known general banner exchanges that you might consider. The best known is Microsoft bCentral's LinkExchange.

The bCentral LinkExchange
http://www.bcentral.com/?leindex
This is an excellent general service that allows you to determine the kind of advertisers you would like on your site. Through its LinkExchange Banner Network you can create a banner advertisement and have the chance to advertise on 450,000 different web sites, in 32 languages, free. You can target your ads by site content and language.

UK Banners
http://www.ukbanners.com/
A similar service dedicated to the UK is UK Banners, a free advertising network dedicated to the UK web community. They say: 'By including some HTML text in your web pages, you show banners advertising other UK web sites In turn, for every 10 times you show a banner on your web pages, your banner is shown 8 times on other UK Banners

More free online promotion

Fig. 50. UK Banners can get your web site noticed in the UK.

member sites (making it one of the highest ratio sites in the UK).' They say that their network is used by over 10,000 web sites around the country, serving in excess of 10 million banners per month. The site offers real-time hourly, daily and weekly graphs and statistics of page impressions, banner exposures, click-throughs and ratios.

Whichever service you use, you'll need to prepare your banner advertisement in advance. You can find advice on designing banners at the Web Marketing Info Center at:

Wilson Web
http://www.wilsonweb.com/webmarket/ad.htm
This is an established and well-known web site for online marketing. You will find a mass of tips and advice about doing business on the net, with hundreds of articles, and more than 2,000 links to resources on e-commerce and web marketing. The site has arranged its subject matter into more than 40 different categories, and grouped materials within these topics for quick accessibility.

Maximising your free publicity

It is always worth thinking about ways in which you can use banners, press releases or email newsletters to improve your publicity.

(a) For instance, the press releases you submit may well be worth extending into an article for inclusion in your email newsletter.

(b) Equally, you can add your banner to your newsletter to allow people to click directly through to your site.

More free online promotion

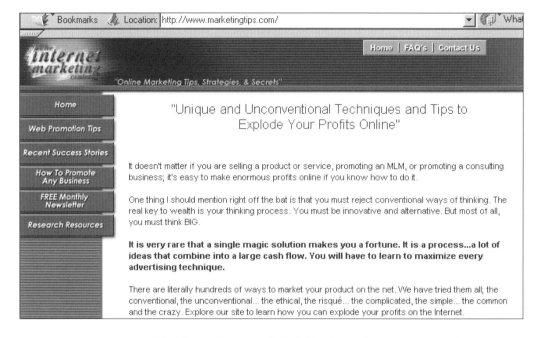

Fig. 51. The Internet Marketing Center has plenty of expert hints and tips to help you promote your site more effectively.

(c) A further 'crossover' of this kind is to submit your press release, an article, or even your banner, to newsletters produced by other people.

There is a healthy exchange of material like this throughout the web. The result is more publicity for your web site and an increased number of links to your pages, thus improving search engine ranking.

Web sites are also looking for 'content' such as your press release or your article, so submitting your material to other web sites for possible inclusion can be worthwhile. All you need do is send your material to the webmaster at each site you would like to include your information. Sometimes you'll get a no-thank-you, other times you will be asked for more details.

There are also information exchange systems where you can upload your content so that other people can use it free of charge at their web sites or in their email newsletters. You can submit your material to a range of sites, including:

Making Profit
http://www.makingprofit.com
Making Profit describes itself as the largest business and marketing article archive on the internet. It features The InfoZone, a searchable archive providing a home for more than 2,600 business and marketing articles about online commerce.

Idea Marketers
http://www.ideamarketers.com/

More free online promotion

Fig. 52. The home page of Idea Marketers offers some useful starting points.

Ensuring successful free promotion

If there is a motto of the successful web site promoter, it must be: 'Persistence Pays'. Sending out just one press release or a couple of targeted emails and the occasional newsletter will be worthless. You need to establish a proper campaign with regular press releases, frequent emails and a strict schedule of newsletters. Add to that the need to upload your free content from these activities to a range of other web sites and you can see that the free publicity is not free after all. You will have devoted a considerable amount of time to the task. However, this effort will pay off in greater traffic directed towards your site.

It is always worth remembering that your site will only be successful if lots of people know about it and are not allowed to forget it exists. With new web sites being added to the internet every minute of every day, you run the definite risk of becoming lost in the crowd unless you are relentless with your promotion.

6 Paying for online promotion

In this chapter we will explore:

▶ *paying for search engine listings*
▶ *paying for online adverts*
▶ *paying for targeted email announcements*
▶ *paying for online public relations activities*
▶ *paying for referrals*
▶ *weighing up the fee-based services*

A significant slice of online promotion is free. You can submit your site to search engines or add your address to directories, and you only need to give up your time to do that. Indeed, if you follow the advice at the Internet Marketing Center (http://www.marketingtips.com/) you'll discover that it is possible to produce a web site in two days, spend two weeks promoting it and then sit back earning thousands of pounds each week for little more than an hour or two of maintenance.

Such success stories are few and far between. The major online successes have come about as a result of money being spent on promotion. It is true you can have a flourishing site without spending any cash, but you will be even more successful if you do. In the online world there are five principal items you pay for which will boost your site. You can:

Fig. 53. You can add your site on Galaxy, one of the earliest and largest internet directories and search engines.

1. pay for search engine listings
2. pay for online advertising

Paying for online promotion

3. pay for targeted email announcements
4. pay for online public relations activities
5. pay for referrals

In addition, of course, you can pay promotional companies to do all of the work on your behalf. Some of the site submission services mentioned in Chapter 2 will provide this kind of additional facility, on top of their free listing services.

Paying for search engine listings

Search engines have not been slow in realising that there is money to be made from guaranteeing a listing or placing your name at the top of the list. The charges that are made vary considerably and sometimes you won't even know how much you'll be charged. That's because you'll be charged an agreed amount 'per impression'.

An 'impression' is the publication of your web site name in a list of possible web site addresses returned to someone making a search. Hence the more people whose searches return your web site name, the higher your fee. At just one cent per impression, it might not sound much. But with trillions of searches being made each week, just imagine what your bill might be if yours is a popular search term. Only 10,000 searches need to return your 'pay by impression' web site address and you will have to pay $1,000 – without any guarantee that any of those people will have clicked through to your site.

Pay-by-impression services are therefore best reserved for large sites with huge incomes who can afford big bills. Nevertheless, the paid-for services in some of the search engines are worthwhile.

Galaxy
http://www.galaxy.com/cgi-bin/annotate?/galaxy
The Galaxy search engine (figure 53) can offer a guaranteed review of your site within 30 days for $25. This way your site, if it is acceptable, gets listed much more quickly than a free submission. If speed of listing is important, this fee may be worth paying.

GoTo
http://www.goto.com
GoTo is a search engine that only lists people who pay. You can sign up for one of three parts of the search engine:

1. the web search
2. the shopping search
3. the auction search

The payment you make will depend on the number of people who click through to your web site.

Unlike pay-per-impression search services, GoTo uses a pay-per-click system. This means you only get charged if someone clicks on your name in a GoTo search list to get to your site. You can also determine the amount

Paying for online promotion.............................

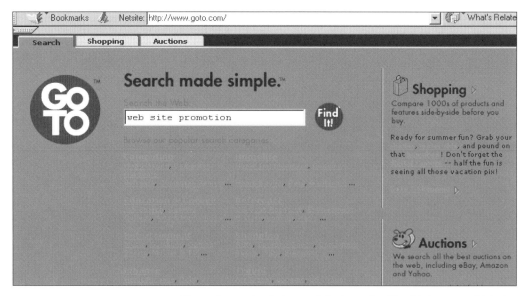

Fig. 54. The search engine you pay for – GoTo.com.

you will pay for each of these click-throughs. The higher your bid, the further up the search list your site will appear – you pay more money for greater prominence. Your bid can be as low as one cent, or as high as you like.

You have to deposit at least $25 with GoTo. You can then decide either to make your promotional work unlimited or that you will spend up to a maximum amount. With unlimited promotional spend, you will keep on paying – the more click-throughs you get, the more you pay. However, the fixed budget plan allows you to set a limit on your spending. Once your money is spent, though, your web site address drops out of any searches.

looksmart

The global leader in search infrastructure, LookSmart provides quality search solutions to leading portals, media companies and ISPs around the world.

For Businesses and Webmasters
Submit your Web site to the LookSmart network and reach 77 percent of US Web users. Enable your site with Beseen and ITW.

LookSmart
http://www.looksmart.com
If your web site is business-related, you can pay LookSmart $299 which will guarantee that your site will be listed within 48 hours, compared with the six to eight weeks of most other search engines. For most businesses this cost will be easily repaid with considerable numbers of extra hits. Paying for LookSmart will also boost your listing at Excite.

Yahoo! Business Express
http://docs.yahoo.com/info/suggest/busexpress.html
If you are running a business, Yahoo! offers a rapid service known as Business Express For a fee of $199 ($600 for adult sites) your web site will be given priority treatment and reviewed within a week. This is all you are buying – payment does not guarantee inclusion, merely a more rapid assessment. For businesses who are confident they will be listed, however, this may well be worthwhile.

Paying for online advertising

Adverts are everywhere on the web and even though many of them

Paying for online promotion

appear free of charge, paying for placement often produces better results, because you can specify where and how often your advert will appear. With free advertising you do not get much say in your campaign.

On the internet, there are as many different ways of advertising as you could imagine. New varieties pop up almost daily. You can pay for:

(a) search-related adverts

(b) banner adverts

(c) pop-up adverts

(d) text-based adverts

(e) email adverts

Search-related adverts
All search engines offer advertising packages. You can have banner adverts on all the search engines which appear when people search for a topic associated with your site. Such people will be more receptive to your advert, as it relates to something they are interested in at that moment. You can find out more about this at each search engine. However, in mid-2000, the minimum cost of this kind of advertising was $1,500 per month. You can get cheaper search-engine advertising, but it will not have the same impact as search-related banners. To learn more about low-cost advertising on search engines go to Microsoft bCentral at:

Microsoft bCentral
http://store.bcentral.com/
Here you will discover that you can advertise on search engines for as little as $50 – but remember, you get what you pay for!

Fig. 55. bCentral is a Microsoft online business service. This is its Advertising Store.

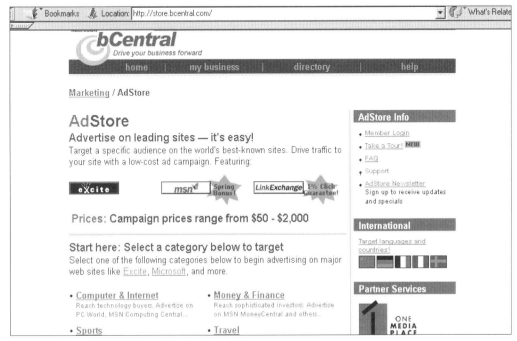

Paying for online promotion..

Paying for pop-ups
Some sites now use pop-up advertisements or floating toolbars packed with adverts. These are small extra windows that appear when you open up a particular web site. The advantage for web site owners is that the advertising does not crowd the design of their own pages. In addition, the advertising window can continually change providing new advertisements, even though the viewer has not moved from the main page. This can bring in extra revenue for the web site publisher.

The danger with pop-up advertising is that it can annoy web site readers. For this reason you can now find a host of 'pop-up killers' – these are programs that monitor incoming web sites and automatically close the pop-up window, so you are not disturbed. This therefore limits the potential for pop-up advertising.

Nevertheless, many sites incorporate this technique and you can buy space in these pop-ups to promote your own site. To find sites you might wish to advertise on you'll need to conduct a search. Just look for the topics you wish to locate and add 'pop-up' to the search terms like this:

    Internet+handbooks+paperbacks+pop-ups

Once you have found somewhere to place your pop-up you'll need a design.

Popup Exchange
http://www.popupexchange.com/designers.htm
You can find a specialist pop-up design service here. They say: 'You can now have a professional pop-up banner/window created for your company for as little as $59.95 (animated $89.95).' It comes with a new talking feature that will tell consumers to click on it. The site includes a portfolio of pop-ups that you can browse through.

DoubleClick
http://www.doubleclick.com
You can also find a useful set of resources about online advertising of all kinds at DoubleClick, one of the best-known sites of its kind.

Taking up text adverts
Text-based advertising is extremely powerful. Your link is hidden within a piece of text. When people click on this text, they are transported to your site. Take a look at this example:

    <A HREF="http://www.web-source.net/"> The Webmasters Resource Directory offers hundreds of thousands of quality resources to assist the small business entrepreneur in designing, marketing and promoting their web sites, products and services. </A>

What this piece of HTML text does is reveal the text between

    >

and

    </A>

Paying for online promotion

The text at the beginning, after < A HREF, is invisible to the user. However, if they click on the text, it will link them to the web site whose name is hidden.

The value of this method is the non-promotional appearance of the link. Because it is text-based, it appears independent and much more authoritative. Text-based advertising is therefore extremely powerful. Not many sites yet offer text-based advertisements, as the banner ad has been so popular, but more and more people are seeing the value of incorporating links into text and publishers are gearing up to provide such services. To find possible text-based advertising for your specific subject area you will need to use a search engine to conduct an advanced search.

Extracting value from email advertisements
You can advertise in a host of email newsletters and ezines. Your advert is usually a short piece of text with your web site address. This could be used to announce your site. Just include a link and use this short advert in ezines that are associated with your specific subject area. You can find a directory of ezines at E-zinez:

E-zinez
http://www.e-zinez.com/

Lifestyles Publishing
http://www.lifestylespub.com/
You can also find a directory of email newsletters and ezines at Lifestyle publishing. They say: 'The Directory of Ezines is a listing of hundreds of ezines that accept advertising. We have found these ezines for you and have also gathered and compiled all of the pertinent advertising information that you would need in order to place your ad for your business opportunity, product or service in any one of the ezines you select.'

Fig. 56. E-zines can help you track down suitable email newsletters that you can use to help promote your site.

Paying for online promotion..

Ezine advertising is very cost effective. A single ad costs around $25 to $30, and research shows that text adverts in emails have significant response rates. Getting your site advertised in ezines should therefore represent good value for money.

Paying for targeted emails

Advertising in ezines is great, but your text can get lost among all the other material. The only way to be sure that your text in an email stands out is to isolate it. You can do this by sending an email that is just about your site.

You can send out targeted emails on your own, free of charge, but it can take time to develop a reasonable size list. There are plenty of sites selling email address lists which you can use to target a specific audience. Most of these services charge around $0.20 per name, which means an email sent to 10,000 potential viewers of your site will cost $2,000. Most of the bulk email providers have a minimum charge of around $500. There are several different targeted email providers including:

Bullet Mail
http://www.bulletmail.com/
As an example, this site recently featured an introductory offer by which you could email your message to 2,000 people for $400, including the actual emailing of your message. You can choose from a selection of more than 100 different targeted opt-in email lists covering a broad range of interests and subject matter.

Electronic Direct Marketing
http://www.edmarketing.com/
They say: 'We are in the business of utilising opt-in email marketing, copy-writing, web design, hosting, maintenance and positioning to deliver your offer where it will get the best attention possible. Let EDM analyse your existing internet strategy and jump in with a custom business package that really delivers.'

Leads Link
http://www.leads-link.com/
Using LeadsLink opt-in lists could help ensure that your message only reaches people who want it, not random internet users whose email addresses were harvested against their will. 'Because we only mail to people who are interested in your products or services, you will get a higher response rate than if you simply emailed everybody.'

PostMaster Direct
http://www.postmasterdirect.com/
Postmaster Direct claims to have the largest network of targeted opt-in email addresses on the internet – more than 3,000 topical lists and 10 million names to choose from. Its partner sites include Cnet, Uproar, ICQ, Internet.com, CBS Sportsline, About.com, CMPnet, Entrepreneur Magazine and many others.

Paying for online promotion

Fig. 57. Postmaster Direct is a site well worth exploring if you want to send out targeted email.

Copywriter
http://www.copywriter.com/lists/
You can also find a directory of email list services here.

Paying for online public relations activities

There are a number of public relations agencies that will send your press releases to journalists for a fee. Many of these are companies that provide everything from online 'wire services' to targeted emails to journalists and broadcasters. The best-known companies are:

Business Wire
http://www.businesswire.com/
Established as a traditional business media service for more than 40 years, Business Wire says it was the first newswire to establish an internet service in 1995. It delivers breaking news and multimedia content to traditional and online newsrooms, targeted journalists, corporate desktops, home PCs, and the new generation of wireless applications. With content from more than 40,000 organisations, Business Wire says it delivers more news from more sources to more destinations than any other service in the world.

Internet News Bureau
http://www.newsbureau.com/
The firm's press-release services enable its clients to reach journalists in both English and non-English speaking countries. Its international media relations partners translate and localise press releases into their native languages, and distribute them to their personal media contacts by email and in some cases by fax and postal mail. The site includes some tips for press-release writing and effective media relations.

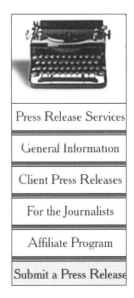

87

Paying for online promotion..

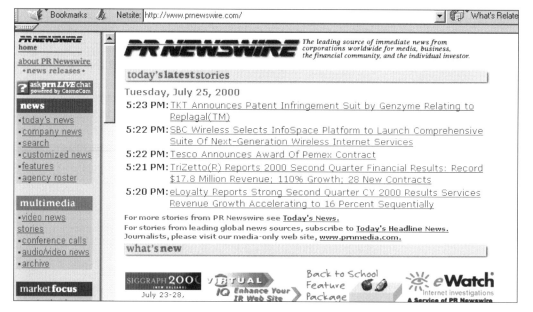

Fig. 58. PR Newswire is a useful facility for international press release distribution.

Press Release Network
http://www.pressreleasenetwork.com
Press Release Network can broadcast your press release to targeted geographic and industry-specific online news agencies and print publications. Press releases distributed by PRN have been published by AFP, Associated Press, Bloomberg, Dow Jones Interactive Publishing, Excite News, Internet Business News, Lexis-Nexis, Reuters, Yahoo News, M2 Presswire and many other global news agencies and online services.

PR Newswire
http://www.prnewswire.com/
PR Newswire offers broadly-based public relations and investor relations services ranging from internet monitoring and information distribution to video news release production and the creation of investor relations web sites and online multimedia content. It says that its wire, fax, satellite and internet network is capable of both pinpoint and mass distribution, satisfying the growing global demand for the immediate delivery of news releases and photos to the media, financial community and consumers.

Xpress Press
http://www.xpresspress.com/
Since 1995, Xpress Press has supplied US and international arts, business and public relations subscribers with a personalised, same-day, distribution network by email. Its media contacts have asked to receive its feed. Each press release sent through its network would be a full-text version of your story. Your wire distribution will have a descriptive email subject header so that reporters can quickly evaluate the content of the release. Xpress Press says that more than 9,000 reporters covering more than 400 news-beats in 36 countries subscribe to its feed.

.... Paying for online promotion

Although charges and services vary, expect to pay around £200 for the distribution of a press release announcing your site to key journalists and publications.

Paying for referrals

There are two ways you can pay to achieve extra traffic directed to your site. One is by developing your own affiliate programme; the other is by using a unique service that was used by Amazon.com.

Affiliate programmes
An affiliate programme is a concept whereby other web sites promote your web site, usually with a graphic link, and you pay them for every person who visits your site as a result of their promotion. It is not a lot different from the 'pay-per-click' advertising of some search engines but, with an affiliate programme you can extend the options for your advertising.

For example, the web sites who become your affiliates could offer particular items that you sell or services you want to promote. You then allow certain kinds of sites to promote specific items. This means that an affiliate programme is much more controllable than simple pay-per-click advertising. Also, if you do sell things on your web site, an affiliate programme simply provides you with more outlets.

Setting up an affiliate programme requires time and an excellent database with good data collection controls. If such a system is not in place, you will not be able to properly allocate payments to each of your affiliates.

Ecommerce Research Room
http://wilsonweb.com/research/associate.htm
You can find out more about setting up an affiliate programme at the Ecommerce Research Room.

Here are some web sites that can help you set up your own affiliate programme:

Be Free
http://www.befree.com/
Through business-to-consumer and business-to-business affiliate marketing channels and hosted, real-time personalisation services, Be Free says that it will help its customers to extend brand reach, drive qualified traffic, generate leads, enhance conversion and increase sales. Be Free is a Nasdaq-quoted company.

Commission Junction
http://www.cj.com/go.asp?69320
Founded in 1998, Commission Junction is a business-to-business web-based sales distribution network that seeks to match online merchants' products and services to online content at the consumer's point-of-interest. It audits ecommerce activity, and collects and pays commissions on sales generated. Commission Junction pays online content sites when a

Paying for online promotion..

Fig. 59. The web site of Link Share is well worth exploring.

customer takes a measurable action, such as a request for information, subscription or purchase.

LinkShare
http://www.linkshare.com/

Revenue Avenue
http://revenue.bcentral.com/
You can search its directory to locate the right programs for you and start earning money from your web site almost at once. You search for the right programs, select the ones you want to join, and use the Express Join facility to apply. The service is operated by Microsoft bCentral.

Specialist referrals
If you want to ensure that your web site announcement reaches people who matter, there is a unique service that was used by Amazon.com to announce its site. Run by Eric Ward from his hillside home in Tennessee, it is called URL Wire.

URL Wire
http://www.urlwire.com
URL Wire provides targeted announcements direct to site reviewers, journalists and other influential people who can help get your site noticed. Eric's system does not depend upon the automation services offered by many site announcement programmes. His is unique because it sends details of your site to the people who will really want to know about it. Hence the targeting of your site announcement is based upon handpicking the people who will be of most use to you. The cost of the service

Paying for online promotion

varies according to your precise requirements but will be between $695 and $1,495.

Fig. 60. URL Wire offers some useful promotional resources.

Weighing up the fee-based services

There are plenty of services on the internet offering to help promote your web site. Before you part with your cash, make sure that the people you are planning to use meet these criteria:

1. There is a professional look to their site.
2. Full contact details listed on their site.
3. They offer a variety of methods of payment.
4. Secure online payment options are available.
5. They can provide references from satisfied customers.
6. They can provide an in-depth report of what they have done on your behalf.

Sites that will not provide references or give reports of their activities are best avoided. They may look good, but how do you know they have actually done the work you have paid for? Finally, you are in a better position to cope with difficulties if you pay by credit card, since you can involve the credit card company in any dispute you have with the firm who sold you their service.

Visit the free Internet HelpZone at
www.internet-handbooks.co.uk
Helping you master the internet

7 Promotion outside the internet

In this chapter we will explore:

▶ *ways of promoting your web site offline*
▶ *advertising contacts*
▶ *direct mail contacts*
▶ *public relations contacts*
▶ *general marketing contacts*
▶ *the importance of word of mouth*
▶ *becoming the best*

Promoting your web site can be time consuming, but exciting and fascinating. As you travel around the web looking at all the different ways you can get publicity for your site you'll stumble across new ideas, interesting insights and brilliant suggestions. However, it is all too easy to get overtaken by the wonderment of everything that you discover. This could mean you'll forget there is a 'real world' outside the internet.

Here are some facts to keep uppermost in mind:

1. Most people are *not* connected to the internet.

2. Surveys have shown that most people find web site addresses from printed media (like this book!).

3. Researchers have produced ample evidence that word-of-mouth recommendation is the most powerful form of advertising.

4. The most successful web sites in the world have spent far more on advertising outside the internet than they have on the web

If you want to ensure that as many people as possible visit your web site, these are very important points to keep in mind. No matter how successful and innovative you have been with your online promotional efforts, do not risk neglecting methods of gaining publicity offline. If you do, your web site will not attract anywhere near the amount of attention it could.

Ways of promoting your web site offline

There are several methods of promoting your web site outside the internet. Essentially, they all fall into the general category of marketing. You are marketing your web site, just as if it were any other product or service. As marketers will tell you, the best campaigns are those based on a strong brand. Your offline activities should reflect the branding you have done with your web site at the outset. Use the logos in your printed advertising, for instance, and add any straplines you use to your business letterheads and other stationery.

.... Promotion outside the internet

Your offline marketing offensive should incorporate the following elements:

(a) consistent printed brand image – headed paper, business cards etc.

(b) direct mail

(c) print advertising

(d) public relations activities

Each of these items will allow your web site address to be more widely disseminated.

One particular point worth noting is that the national press continues to be full of stories about the internet, and many newspapers now have weekly supplements on the web. In addition, there are now many monthly magazines about the internet, as well as a host of computer magazines devoted to web-related topics.

All this editorial space needs filling – hence your press releases and articles will be welcomed, provided they offer something of real value to readers and not mere puffery for your site. Do not neglect this avenue of publicity, as it will increase the chances of having your web site address widely noticed.

▶ *Contact* – You can find the addresses of UK newspapers and magazines in *Editors* from Media Information Limited, telephone 01494 797230.

Advertising contacts

You might not wish to afford a national advertising campaign, but a targeted series of advertisements in a trade magazine, for instance, may be all you need to increase awareness of your sites. The long-established reference publication *Willings Press Guide* contains details of UK magazines which can accept your adverts. To find out more, contact Willings at Hollis Directories, telephone 020 8977 7711.

Advertising Standards Authority
http://www.asa.org.uk/
The ASA exists to ensure the standards of non-broadcast advertisements in the UK. Its site contains the British Codes of Advertising, plus various research items and a database of adjudications on complaints.

Advertising Standards Authority for Ireland
http://www.asai.ie
This is an independent body set up and financed by the Irish advertising industry.

Institute of Practitioners in Advertising
http://www.ipa.co.uk/
Founded in 1917, this is the home page of the London-based IPA, the professional body for UK advertising agencies. The site contains details of

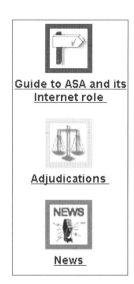

Promotion outside the internet

its membership, together with a resources centre. You need to complete an online registration form to access the information available. You are then given guest status. Certain areas of the site, such as Services, are available to IPA member agencies only, for which member status is required.

Direct mail contacts

Direct Marketing Association
http://www.the-dma.org/
The DMA provides information and services both to direct marketers and to consumers. It is the oldest and largest UK trade association for users and suppliers in the direct, database and interactive marketing fields.

Fig. 61. The home page of the UK Direct Marketing Association (DMA).

Public relations contacts

Institute of Public Relations
http://www.ipr.org.uk/
The IPR is the professional organisation for the UK PR industry, offering careers training and membership information. It is also the largest individual member public relations society in Europe. The web site includes a list of PR industry related and other useful websites.

International Public Relations Association
http://www.ipranet.org
IPRA has a membership drawn from more than 70 countries.

Promotion outside the internet

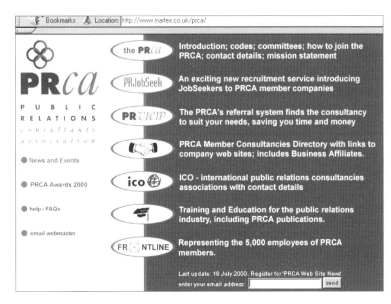

Fig. 62. The home page of the Public Relations Consultants Association (PRCA).

Public Relations Consultants Association
http://www.martex.co.uk/prca/
The PRCA offers a recruitment service, referral system, news, industry training, and consultancies.

General marketing contacts

Chartered Institute of Marketing
http://www.cim.co.uk/
This is a key information resource for UK marketing and sales professionals. The authoritative and substantial web site contains details of its membership, numerous professional and training services, resources and news.

Fig. 63. The home page of the Chartered Institute of Marketing (CIM), the leading membership and training organisation for professional marketers in the UK.

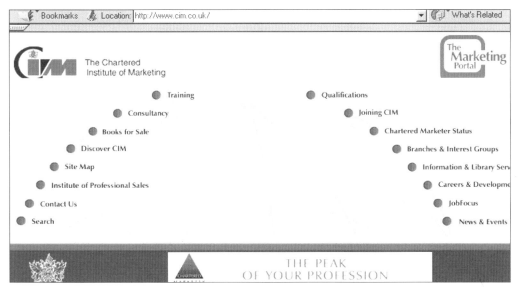

Promotion outside the internet

Institute of Sales Promotion
http://www.isp.org.uk
The ISP is dedicated to protecting and promoting the UK sales promotion industry.

Market Research Society
http://www.marketresearch.org.uk/
Based in the City of London, the Market Research Society is the world's largest professional body for individuals employed in market research or just interested in the subject. It provides a comprehensive range of publications, information and advisory services, training courses, conferences, seminars and networking opportunities.

The importance of word of mouth

Word-of-mouth advertising is very powerful. Personal recommendations of web sites are an extremely common way of people finding out about them. You should therefore use every opportunity to encourage word-of-mouth advertising.

1. Consider attending trade shows, exhibitions and other events and functions to promote a business site. The Tradeworld Exhibition Centre web site, for example, has access to regularly updated information on exhibitions, trade fairs, expositions and shows:

    http://www.tradeworld.co.uk/exhibitions/

2. Go to hobby exhibitions or sports centres for sites associated with leisure activities. In fact, any way in which you can meet the very people who may well be your viewers is ideal. They will learn about the site from you and may well pass on the information.

If your web site has a snappy and easy-to-remember domain name, it will boost the ease with which word-of-mouth advertising can happen. The internet can do a lot to promote your site, but there is nothing to beat getting out there amongst the people who'll be your viewers – it works wonders. That's why many big businesses have road shows and events to bring them face-to-face with their customers. It helps them learn about how they can improve their products, but it also helps boost the likelihood of word-of-mouth advertising. Follow their example, and get as much free publicity of this kind as you can.

Becoming the best

If you really want to become one of the world's most popular web sites, you are going to have to spend a lot of money, and most of that will be spent offline. You will need to be at seminars and exhibitions, on posters and hoardings, in newspapers and magazines and on as many chat shows on TV as you can. You'll probably need a celebrity or two for good measure! The big names we all know – Yahoo!, Amazon, Lastminute, etc – have all spent millions on advertising and public relations.

Promotion outside the internet

A web site, like any other product, is only as effective as the promotion it receives. The more you promote your web site, the more effective it will become. However, with the millions of web sites all competing for the same kind of audiences, promotion is more important than for other products.

▶ *Key strategy* – The successful web site is the one that is willing to spend a much higher proportion of its time and money on promotional activity than a comparable offline enterprise.

List of web sites

AdStore Central	http://store.bcentral.com/
Advertising Marketing & Promotional Services	http://www.amps-inc.com/awards.html
Aleph Search	http://www.albedo.co.uk/sites/aleph/
All Search Engines	http://www.allsearchengines.co.uk/
AltaVista add URL	http://www.uni-karlsruhe.de/~un9v/atm/ase.html
Amazon	http://www.amazon.com
Anti Spam Directory	http://www.dgl.com/docs/antispam.html
Ask Jeeves add URL	http://www.askjeeves.com/docs/about/policy.html
Banner Exchanges	http://www.bxmegalist.com/
Banner Warehouse	http://www.stuff.uk.com/banners/index.shtml
bCentral	http://www.bcentral.com/
Be Free	http://www.befree.com
Bullet Mail	http://www.bulletmail.com/
Business Wire	http://www.businesswire.com/
Clip Art	http://www.clipart.co.uk
Coalition Against Unsolicited Commercial Email	http://www.cauce.org/
Commission Junction	http://www.cj.com/go.asp?69320
CopyWriter	http://www.copywriter.com/lists/
Cyber Eye	http://www.meta-tags.com
Data Protection Commissioner	http://www.dataprotection.gov.uk/dprhome.htm
Design Consultants Directory	http://www.designdirectory.co.uk/
Dir of Dirs	http://www.gmilne.demon.co.uk/engines.htm
Domain Name News	http://www.domain-name-news.com
Double Click	http://www.doubleclick.com
E-boz	http://www.eboz.com/advice/banner_advertising/
Ecommerce Research Room	http://wilsonweb.com/research/associate.htm
Electronic Direct Marketing	http://www.edmarketing.com/
Excite add URL	http://www.excite.co.uk/info/add.url
Exploit Submission Wizard	http://www.exploit.net/wizard/index.html
E-zinez	http://www.e-zinez.com/
Galaxy paid entries	http://www.galaxy.com/cgi-bin/annotate?/galaxy
Google add URL	http://www.google.com/addurl.html
GoTo	http://www.goto.com
Great Promote	http://www.greatpromote.com/guide/stucker.html
GW Web Design	http://gwwebdesign.com
HG Marketing	http://www.hgmarketing.com/articles/freepub2.shtml
Hi Verify	http://www.hisoftware.com/verify.htm
Hot Bot	http://www.hotbot.com
Idea Marketers	http://www.ideamarketers.com/
InfoSeek add URL	http://www.infoseek.com/AddUrl?pg=DCaddurl.html&sv=UK
Internet Handbooks	http://www.internet-handbooks.co.uk
Internet News Bureau	http://www.newsbureau.com/
Intersaver	http://www.intersaver.co.uk
JavaScrip Pop Ups	http://grahamjones.net/java.htm
Leads Link	http://www.leads-link.com/
Lifestyle	http://www.lifestylespub.com/
Link Exchange	http://www.bcentral.com/?leindex
Link Share	http://www.linkshare.com
ListBot	http://www.listbot.com/
LookSmart	http://www.looksmart.com
Lycos	http://www.lycos.co.uk
Making Profit	http://www.makingprofit.com

List of web sites

Matt's Script Archive	http://www.worldwidemart.com/scripts/links.shtml
Media First	http://www.mediafirst.co.uk
Metabot	http://www.tetranetsoftware.com/products/metabot.htm
MSN add URL	http://search.msn.co.uk/addurl.asp
Name A Dot Com	http://www.name-a.com
NerdWorld	http://www.nerdworld.com/nwadd.html
NetMechanic	http://www.netmechanic.com
Onlin Biz Promote	http://online-biz.com/promote/
Open Directory Project	http://dmoz.org/
Page Submit Pro	http://www.pagesubmit.com
PopUp Exchange	http://www.popupexchange.com/designers.htm
PostMaster Direct	http://www.postmasterdirect.com/
PR Newswire	http://www.prnewswire.com/
PR Web	http://www.prweb.com
Press Release Network	http://www.pressreleasenetwork.com
Press Release Writing	http://www.press-release-writing.com
ProBoost	http://www.proboost.com/
Reciprocal links	http://www.reciprocallink.com/
Revenue Avenue	http://revenue.bcentral.com/
Scoot	http://www.scoot.co.uk
ScrubTheWeb add URL	http://www.scrubtheweb.com/addurl.html
Search Engine Colossus	http://www.searchenginecolossus.com/
Search Engine Watch	http://www.searchenginewatch.com/
Searchability	http://www.searchability.com/index.htm
Site Promoting	http://www.site-promoting.co.uk
Snap	http://www.snap.com
SoftSeek	http://www.softseek.com
Submit Corner	http://www.submitcorner.com/Tools/Meta/
Submit It	http://submitit.bcentral.com/
Submit URL	http://www.submit-url.net/
Submit Wolf	http://www.trellian.com/swolf/index.html
The E-zine Factory	http://www.ezinefactory.co.za/infopages/ezines.htm
The Internet Marketing Center	http://www.marketingtips.com/
The Web Wire	http://www.webwire.com
The Web Writer	http://www.the-web-writer.co.uk
Traffic Builder	http://www.intelliquis.com/products/traffic.stm
UK Banners	http://www.ukbanners.com/
UK Plus	http://www.ukplus.co.uk
URL Wire	http://www.urlwire.com
Web Marketing Info Center	http://www.wilsonweb.com/webmarket/ad.htm
Web Metrics	http://www.wwwmetrics.com/
Web Position Gold	http://www.webpositiongold.com/
Web Reference	http://www.webreference.com/dlab/
Web Ring	http://www.webring.org/#ringworld
WebCrawler add URL	http://www.webcrawler.com/info/add.url/
Webs Unlimited	http://www.websunlimited.com/
WhatsNu	http://www.whatsnu.com/
Xpress Press	http://www.xpresspress.com/
Yahoo	http://www.yahoo.com
Yale Style Guide	http://info.med.yale.edu/caim/manual/
Yellow Pages	http://www.yellowpages.co.uk/Aboutus

Glossary of internet terms

access provider – The company that provides you with access to the internet. This may be an independent provider or a large international organisation such as AOL or CompuServe. See also **internet service provider**.

ActiveX – A programming language that allows effects such as animations, games and other interactive features to be included a web page.

Adobe Acrobat – A type of software required for reading PDF files ('portable document format'). You may need to have Adobe Acrobat Reader when downloading large text files from the internet, such as lengthy reports or chapters from books. If your computer lacks it, the web page will prompt you, and usually offer you an immediate download of the free version.

address book – A directory in a web browser where you can store people's email addresses. This saves having to type them out each time you want to email someone. You just click on an address whenever you want it.

ADSL – Advanced digital subscriber line.

Adult check – An age verification system that only allows the over 18s to enter adult web sites.

affiliate programme – A system that allows you to sell other companies products via your web site.

age verification – Commercial systems that prevent minors from accessing adult oriented web sites.

AltaVista – One of the half dozen most popular internet search engines. Just type in a few key words to find what you want on the internet. See: – http://www.altavista.com

AOL – America On Line, the world's biggest internet service provider, with more than 20 million subscribers, and now merged with Time Warner. Because it has masses of content of its own – quite aside from the wider internet – it is sometimes referred to as an 'online' service provider rather than internet service provider. It has given away vast numbers of free CDs with the popular computer magazines to build its customer base. See: – http://www.aol.com

Apple Macintosh – A type of computer that has its own proprietary operating system, as distinct from the MSDOS and Windows operating systems found on PCs (personal computers). The Apple Mac has long been a favourite of designers and publishers.

applet – An application programmed in Java that is designed to run only on a web browser. Applets cannot read or write data onto your computer, only from the domain in which they are served from. When a web page using an applet is accessed, the browser will download it and run it on your computer. See also **Java**.

application – Any program, such as a word processor or spreadsheet program, designed for use on your computer.

application service provider – A company that provides computer software via the internet, whereby the application is borrowed, rather than downloaded. You keep your data, they keep the program.

ARPANET – Advanced Research Projects Agency Network, an early form of the internet.

ASCII – American Standard Code for Information Interchange. It is a simple text file format that can be accessed by most word processors and text editors. It is a universal file type for passing textual information across the internet.

Ask Jeeves – A popular internet search engine. Rather than just typing in a few key words for your search, you can type in a whole question or instruction, such as 'Find me everything about online investment.' It draws on a database of millions of questions and answers, and works best with fairly general ques-

Glossary of internet terms

tions.

ASP – (1) Active Server Page, a filename extension for a type of web page. (2) Application service provider (see above),

attachment – A file sent with an email message. The attached file can be anything from a word-processed document to a database, spreadsheet, graphic, or even a sound or video file. For example you could email someone birthday greetings, and attach a sound track or video clip.

Authenticode – Authenticode is a system where ActiveX controls can be authenticated in some way, usually by a certificate.

avatar – A cartoon or image used to represent someone on screen while taking part in internet chat.

backup – A second copy of a file or a set of files. Backing up data is essential if there is any risk of data loss.

bandwidth – The width of the electronic highway that gives you access to the internet. The higher the bandwidth, the wider this highway, and the faster the traffic can flow.

banner ad – This is a band of text and graphics, usually situated at the top of a web page. It acts like a title, telling the user what the content of the page is about. It invites the visitor to click on it to visit that site. Banner advertising has become big business.

baud rate – The data transmission speed in a modem, measured in bps (bits per second).

BBS – Bulletin board service. A facility to read and to post public messages on a particular web site.

binary numbers – The numbering system used by computers. It only uses 1s and 0s to represent numbers. Decimal numbers are based on the number 10. You can count from nought to nine. When you count higher than nine, the nine is replaced with a 10. Binary numbers are based on the number 2: each place can only have the value of 1 or 0.

Blue Ribbon Campaign – A widely supported campaign supporting free speech and opposing moves to censor the internet by all kinds of elected and unelected bodies. See the Electronic Frontier Foundation at: http://www.eff.org

bookmark – A file of URLs of your favourite internet sites. Bookmarks are very easily created by bookmarking (mouse-clicking) any internet page you like the look of. If you are an avid user, you could soon end up with hundreds of them! In the Internet Explorer browser and AOL they are called Favorites.

boolean search – A search in which you type in words such as AND and OR to refine your search. Such words are called 'Boolean operators'. The concept is named after George Boole, a nineteenth-century English mathematician.

bot – Short for robot. It is used to refer to a program that will perform a task on the internet, such as carrying out a search.

brokers – Online agencies that buy and sell domain names.

browser – Your browser is your window to the internet, and will normally supplied by your internet service provider when you first sign up. It is the program that you use to access the world wide web, and manage your personal communications and privacy when online. By far the two most popular browsers are Netscape Communicator and its dominant rival Microsoft Internet Explorer. You can easily swap. Both can be downloaded free from their web sites and are found on the CD roms stuck to the computer magazines. It won't make much difference which one you use – they both do much the same thing. Opera, at http://www.opera.com is a great alternative that improves security, is faster and more efficient. America Online has its own proprietary browser which is not available separately.

bug – A weakness in a program or a computer system.

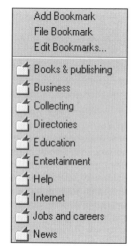

Glossary of internet terms

bulletin board – A type of computer-based news service that provides an email service and a file archive.

cache – A file storage area on a computer. Your web browser will normally cache (copy to your hard drive) each web page you visit. When you revisit that page on the web, you may in fact be looking at the page originally cached on your computer. To be sure you are viewing the current page, press **reload** or **refresh** on your browser toolbar. You can empty your cache from time to time, and the computer will do so automatically whenever the cache is full. In Internet Explorer, pages are saved in the Windows folder, Temporary Internet Files. In Netscape they are saved in a folder called 'cache'.

certificate – A computer file that securely identifies a person or organisation on the internet.

CGI – Common gateway interface. This defines how the web server should pass information to the program, such as what it's being asked to do, what objects it should work with, any inputs, and so on. It is the same for all web servers.

channel (chat) – Place where you can chat with other internet chatters. The name of a chat channel is prefixed with a hash mark, #.

click stream – The sequence of hyperlinks clicked by someone when using the internet.

click through – This is when someone clicks on a banner ad or other link, for example, and is moved from that page to the advertiser's web site.

client – This is the term given to the program that you use to access the internet. For example your web browser is a web client, and your email program is an email client.

colocating – Putting your computer at another company's location so you can connect your web site permanently to the internet.

community – The internet is often described as a net community. This refers to the fact that many people like the feeling of belonging to a group of like-minded individuals. Many big web sites have been developed along these lines, such as GeoCities which is divided into special-interest 'neighbourhoods', or America OnLine which is strong on member services.

compression – Computer files can be electronically compressed, so that they can be uploaded or downloaded more quickly across the internet, saving time and money. If an image file is compressed too much, there may be a loss of quality. To read them, you uncompress 'unzip' them.

content – Articles, columns, sales messages, images, and the text of your web site.

content services – Web sites dedicated to a particular subject.

cookie – A cookie is a small code that the server asks your browser to keep until it asks for it. If it sends it with the first page and asks for it back before each other page, they can follow you around the site, even if you switch your computer off in between.

cracker – Someone who breaks into computer systems with the intention of causing some kind of damage or abusing the system in some way.

crash – What happens when a computer program malfunctions. The operating system of your PC may perform incorrectly or come to a complete stop ('freeze'), forcing you to shut down and restart.

cross-posting – Posting an identical message in several different newsgroups at the same time.

cybercash – This is a trademark, but is also often used as a broad term to describe the use of small payments made over the internet using a new form of electronic account that is loaded up with cash. You can send this money to the companies offering such cash facilities by cheque, or by credit card. Some internet companies offering travel-related items can accept electronic cash of this kind.

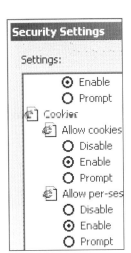

103

Glossary of internet terms

cyberspace – Popular term for the intangible 'place' where you go to surf – the ethereal and borderless world of computers and telecommunications on the internet.

cypherpunk – From the cypherpunk mailing list charter: 'Cypherpunks assume privacy is a good thing and wish there were more of it. Cypherpunks acknowledge that those who want privacy must create it for themselves and not expect governments, corporations, or other large, faceless organisations to grant them privacy out of beneficence. Cypherpunks know that people have been creating their own privacy for centuries with whispers, envelopes, closed doors, and couriers. Cypherpunks do not seek to prevent other people from speaking about their experiences or their opinions.'

cypherpunk remailer – Cypherpunk remailers strip headers from the messages and add new ones.

cybersquatting – Using someone else's name or trademark as your domain name in the hope they will buy it from you

cyberstalker – An individual who pursues you or your children using email, chat rooms and newsgroups. Often attempting to arrange a meeting with children.

data – Information. Data can exist in many forms such as numbers in a spreadsheet, text in a document, or as binary numbers stored in a computer's memory.

database – A store of information in digital form. Many web sites make use of substantial databases to deliver maximum content at high speed to the web user.

dial-up account – This allows you to connect your computer to your internet provider's computer remotely.

digital – Based on the two binary digits, 1 and 0. The operation of all computers is based on this amazingly simple concept. All forms of information are capable of being digitalised – numbers, words, and even sounds and images – and then transmitted over the internet.

digital signature – A unique personal signature specially created for use over the internet, designed to take the place of the traditional handwritten signature.

directory – On a PC, a folder containing your files.

DNS – Domain name server.

domain name – A name that identifies an IP address. It identifies to the computers on the rest of the internet where to access particular information. Each domain has a name. For someone@somewhere.co.uk, 'somewhere' is the domain name. The domain name for Internet Handbooks for instance is: www.internet-handbooks.co.uk

download – Downloading means copying a file from one computer on the internet to your own computer. You do this by clicking on a button that links you to the appropriate file. Downloading is an automatic process, except that you have to click 'yes' to accept the download and give it a file name. You can download any type of file – text, graphics, sound, spreadsheet, computer programs, and so on.

ebusiness – The broad concept of doing business to business, and business to consumer sales, over the internet.

ecash – Short for electronic cash. See cybercash.

Echelon – The name of a massive governmental surveillance facility based in Yorkshire, UK. Operated clandestinely by the USA, UK and certain other governments, it is said to be eavesdropping on virtually the entire traffic of the internet. It is said to use special electronic dictionaries to trawl through millions of emails and other transmissions.

ecommerce – The various means and techniques of transacting business online.

Glossary of internet terms

email – Electronic mail, any message or file you send from your computer to another computer using your 'email client' program (such as Netscape Messenger or Microsoft Outlook).

email address – The unique address given to you by your ISP. It can be used by others using the internet to send email messages to you. An example of a standard email address is:

mybusiness@aol.com

email bomb – An attack by email where you are sent hundreds or thousands of email messages in a very short period. This attack often prevents you receiving genuine email messages.

emoticons – Popular symbols used to express emotions in email, for example the well-known smiley

:-) which means 'I'm smiling!'

Emoticons are not normally appropriate for business communications.

encryption – The scrambling of information to make it unreadable without a key or password. Email and any other data can now be encrypted using PGP and other freely available programs. Modern encryption has become so amazingly powerful as to be to all intents and purposes uncrackable. Law enforcers world wide are pressing their governments for access to people's and organisation's passwords and security keys. Would you be willing to hand over yours?

Excite – A popular internet directory and search engine used to find pages relating to specific keywords which you enter. See http://www.excite.com

ezines – The term for magazines and newsletters published on the internet.

FAQs – Frequently asked questions. You will see 'FAQ' everywhere you go on the internet. If you are ever doubtful about anything check the FAQ page, if the site has one, and you should find the answers to your queries.

favorites – The rather coy term for **bookmarks** used by Internet Explorer, and by America Online. Maintaining a list of 'favourites' is designed to make returning to a site easier.

file – A file is any body of data such as a word processed document, a spreadsheet, a database file, a graphics or video file, sound file, or computer program. On a PC, a file has a filename, and filename extension showing what type of file it is.

filtering software – Software loaded onto a computer to prevent access by someone to unwelcome content on the internet, notably porn. The well-known 'parental controls' include CyberSitter, CyberPatrol, SurfWatch and NetNanny. They can be blunt instruments. For example, if they are programmed to reject all web pages containing the word 'virgin', you would not be able to access any web page hosted at Richard Branson's Virgin Net! Of course, there are also web sites that tell you step-by-step how to disable or bypass these filtering tools, such as: http://www.peacefire.org

finger – A tool for locating people on the internet. The most common use is to see if a person has an account at a particular internet site. Also, a chat command that returns information about the other chat user, including idle time (time since they last did anything).

firewall – A firewall is special security software designed to stop the flow of certain files into and out of a computer network, e.g. viruses or attacks by hackers. A firewall would be an important feature of any fully commercial web site.

flame – A more or less hostile or aggressive message posted in a newsgroup or to an individual newsgroup user. If they get out of hand there can be flame wars.

folder – The name for a directory on a computer. It is a place in which files are stored.

Glossary of internet terms ....

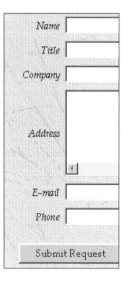

form – A web page that allows or requires you to enter information into fields on the page and send the information to a web site, program or individual on the web. Forms are often used for registration or sending questions and comments to web sites.

forums – Places for discussion on the internet. They include Usenet newsgroups, mailing lists, and bulletin board services.

frames – A web design feature in which web pages are divided into several areas or panels, each containing separate information. A typical set of frames in a page includes an index frame (with navigation links), a banner frame (for a heading), and a body frame (for text matter).

freebies – The 'give away' products, services or other enticements offered on a web site to attract registrations.

freespace – An allocation of free web space by an internet service provider or other organisation, to its users or subscribers.

freeware – Software programs made available without charge. Where a small charge is requested, the term is **shareware**.

front page – The first page of your web site that the visitor will see. FrontPage is also the name of a popular web authoring package from Microsoft.

ftp – File transfer protocol, the method the internet uses to speed files back and forth between computers. Your browser will automatically select this method, for instance, when you want to download your bank statements to reconcile your accounts. In practice you don't need to worry about FTP unless you are thinking about creating and publishing your own web pages: then you would need some of the freely available FTP software. Despite the name, it's easy to use.

gif – Graphic interchange format. It is a widely-used compressed file format used on web pages and elsewhere to display files that contain graphic images. See also **jpg** and **pdf**.

graphical client – A graphical client typically uses many windows, one for each conversation you are involved in. Each window has a command line and status bar.

GUI – Short for graphic user interface. It describes the user-friendly screens found in Windows and other WIMP environments (Windows, icons, mice, pointers).

hacker – A person interested in computer programming, operating systems, the internet and computer security. The term can be used to describe a person who breaks into computer systems with the intention of pointing out the weaknesses in a system. In common usage, the term is often wrongly used to describe crackers.

header – The header is that part of a message which contains information about the sender and the route that the message took through the internet.

history list – A record of visited web pages. Your browser probably includes a history list. It is handy way of revisiting sites whose addresses you have forgotten to bookmark – just click on the item you want in the history list. You can normally delete all or part of the history list in your browser. However, your ISP may well be keeping a copy of this information even if you delete it on your own computer (see **internet service providers**, above).

hit counter – A piece of software used by a web site to publicly display the number of hits it has received.

hits – The number of times a web page has been viewed.

home page – This refers to the index page of an individual or an organisation on the internet. It usually contains links to related pages of information, and to other relevant sites

host – A host is the computer where a particular file or domain is located, and from where people can retrieve it.

HotBot – A popular internet search engine used to find pages relating to any key-

Glossary of internet terms

words you decide to enter.

html – Hyper text markup language, the universal computer language used to create pages on the world wide web. It is much like word processing, but uses special 'tags' for formatting the text and creating hyperlinks to other web pages.

http – Hypertext transfer protocol, the protocol used by the world wide web. It is the language spoken between your browser and the web servers. It is the standard way that HTML documents are transferred from host computer to your local browser when you're surfing the internet. You'll see this acronym at the start of every web address, for example:

>   http://www.abcxyz.com

With modern browsers, it is no longer necessary to enter 'http://' at the start of the address.

hyperlink – See **link**.

hypertext – This is a link on an HTML page that, when clicked with a mouse, results in a further HTML page or graphic being loaded into view on your browser.

IANA The Internet Assigned Numbers Authority, the official body responsible for ensuring that the numerical coding of the internet works properly,

ICANN – The committee that oversees the whole domain name system.

ICQ – A form of internet chat, derived from the phrase 'I seek you'. It enables users to be alerted whenever fellow users go online, so they can have instant chat communication. The proprietary software is now owned by America Online.

impression – An internet advertising term that means the showing of a single instance of an advert on a single computer screen.

Infoseek – One of the ten most popular internet search engines.

Intel – Manufacturer of the Pentium and other microprocessors.

internet – The broad term for the fast-expanding network of global computers that can access each other in seconds by phone and satellite links. If you are using a modem on your computer, you too are part of the internet. The general term 'internet' encompasses email, web pages, internet chat, newsgroups, mailing lists, bulletin boards, and video conferencing. It is rather like the way we speak of 'the printed word' when we mean books, magazines, newspapers, newsletters, catalogues, leaflets, tickets and posters. The 'internet' does not exist in one place any more than 'the printed word' does.

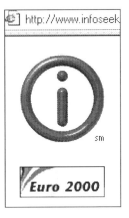

internet2 – A new form of the internet being developed exclusively for educational and academic use.

internet account – The account set up by your internet service provider which gives you access to the world wide web, electronic mail facilities, newsgroups and other value added services.

internet directory – A special web site which consists of information about other sites. The information is classified by subject area and further subdivided into smaller categories. The biggest and most widely used is Yahoo! at: http://www.yahoo.com. See also **search engines**.

Internet Explorer – The world's most popular browser software, a product of Microsoft and leading the field against Netscape (now owned by America Online).

internet keywords – A commercial service that allows people to find your domain name without having to type in www or .com

internet protocol number – The numerical code that is your real domain name address.

internet service providers – ISPs are commercial, educational or official organisations which offer people ('users') access to the internet. The well-known commercial ones in the UK include AOL, CompuServe, BT Internet, Freeserve,

Glossary of internet terms ....

Demon and Virgin Net. Commercial ISPs may levy a fixed monthly charge, though the worldwide trend is now towards free services. Services typically include access to the world wide web, email and newsgroups, as well as others such as news, chat, and entertainment. Your internet service provider will probably know everything you do on the internet – emails sent and received, web sites visited, information downloaded, key words typed into search engines, newsgroups visited and messages read and posted. This is why many of them are willing to offer their services free. What do they do with all this data? How long do they store it? Do they make it discreetly available to government agencies? There are some major issues of personal privacy and data protection in all this, at both a national and European level, and state surveillance is expanding fast. At the very least, check out your service provider's privacy statement but it may mean very little.

intranet – A private computer network that uses internet technology to allow communication between individuals, for example within a large commercial organisation. It often operates on a LAN (local area network).

IP address – An 'internet protocol' address. All computers linked to the internet have one. The address is somewhat like a telephone number, and consists of four sets of numbers separated by dots.

IPv6 – The new internet coding system that will allow even more domain names.

IRC – Internet relay chat. Chat is an enormously popular part of the internet, and there are all kinds of chat rooms and chat software. The chat involves typing messages which are sent and read in real time. It was developed in 1988 by a Finn called Jarkko Oikarinen.

ISDN – Integrated Services Digital Network. This is a high-speed telephone network that can send computer data from the internet to your PC faster than a normal telephone line.

Java – A programming language developed by Sun Microsystems to use the special properties of the internet to create graphics and multimedia applications on web sites.

JavaScript – A simple programming language that can be put onto a web page to create interactive effects such as buttons that change appearance when you position the mouse over them.

jpeg – The acronym is short for Joint Photographic Experts Group. A JPEG or JPG is a specialised file format used to display graphic files on the internet. JPEG files are smaller than similar GIF files and so have become ever more popular – even though there is sometimes a feeling that their quality is not as good as GIF format files. See also MPEG.

key shortcut – Two keys pressed at the same time. Usually the 'control' key (Ctrl), 'Alt' key, or 'Shift' key combined with a letter or number. For example to use 'Control-D', press 'Control', tap the 'D' key once firmly then take your finger off the 'Control' key.

keywords – Words that sum up your web site for being indexed in search engines. For example for a cosmetic site the key words might include beauty, lipstick, make-up, fashion, cosmetic and so on.

kick – To eject someone from a chat channel.

LAN – A local area network, a computer network usually located in one building or campus.

link – A hypertext phrase or image that calls up another web page when you click on it. Most web sites have lots of hyperlinks, or 'links' for short. These appear on the screen as buttons, images or bits of text (often underlined) that you can click on with your mouse to jump to another site on the world wide web.

Linux – A new widely and freely available operating system for personal computers, and a potentially serious challenger to Microsoft. It has developed a considerable following.

Glossary of internet terms

LINX – The London Internet Exchange, the facility which maintains UK internet traffic in the UK. It allows existing individual internet service providers to exchange traffic within the UK, and improve connectivity and service for their customers. LINX is one of the largest and fastest growing exchange points in Europe, and maintains connectivity between the UK and the rest of the world.

listserver – An automated email system whereby subscribers are able to receive and send email from other subscribers to the list.

log on/log off – To access/leave a network. In the early days of computing this literally involved writing a record in a log book. You may be asked to 'log on' to certain sites and particular pages. This normally means entering your user ID in the form of a name and a password.

lurk – The slang term used to describe reading a newsgroup's messages without actually taking part in that newsgroup. Despite the connotations of the word, it is a perfectly respectable activity on the internet.

macros – 'Macro languages' are used to automate repetitive tasks in Word processors and other applications.

mail server – A remote computer that enables you to send and receive emails. Your internet access provider will usually act as your mail server.

mailing list – A forum where messages are distributed by email to the members of the forum. The two types of lists are discussion and announcement. Discussion lists allow exchange between list members. Announcement lists are one-way only and used to distribute information such as news or humour. A good place to find mailing lists is Liszt (http://www.liszt.com). You can normally quit a mailing list by sending an email message to request removal.

marquee – A moving (scrolling) line of text on a web site, normally used for advertising purposes.

Media player – Software on a personal computer that will play sounds and images including video clips and animations.

metasearch engine – A site that sends a keyword search to many different search engines and directories so you can use many search engines from one place.

meta tags The technical term for the keywords used in your web page code to help search engine software rank your site.

Microsoft – The world's biggest producer of software for personal computers, including the Windows operating systems, and the web browser Internet Explorer.

Mixmaster – An anonymous remailer that sends and receives email messages as packages of exactly the same size and often randomly varies the delay time between receiving and remailing to make interception harder.

modem – This is an internal or external piece of hardware plugged into your PC. It links into a standard phone socket, thereby giving you access to the internet. The word derives from MOdulator/DEModulator.

moderator – A person in charge of a mailing list, newsgroup or forum. The moderator prevents unwanted messages.

mpeg or **mpg** – The file format used for video clips available on the internet. See also JPEG.

MP3 – An immensely popular audio format that allows you to download and play music on your computer. It compresses music to create files that are small yet whose quality is almost as good as CD music. See http://mpeg.org for further technical information, or the consumer web site www.mp3.com. At the time of writing, MP4, even faster to download was being developed.

MUDs – Multi-user dungeons, interactive chat-based fantasy world games. Popular in the early days of the internet, they are in now in decline with the advance of networked arcade games such as Quake and Doom.

navigate – To click on the hyperlinks on a web site in order to move to other web

Glossary of internet terms

pages or internet sites.

net – A slang term for the internet. In the same way, the world wide web is often just called the web.

netiquette – Popular term for the unofficial rules and language people follow to keep electronic communication in an acceptably polite form.

Netmeeting – This Microsoft plug in allows a moving video picture to be contained within a web page. It is now integrated into Windows Media Player.

Netscape – After Microsoft's Internet Explorer, Netscape is the most popular browser software available for surfing the internet. An excellent product, Netscape has suffered in the wake of Internet Explorer, mainly because of the success of Microsoft in getting the latter pre-loaded on most new PCs. Netscape Communicator comes complete with email, newsgroups, address book and bookmarks, plus a web page composer, and you can adjust its settings in all sorts of useful ways. Netscape was taken over by American Online for $4 billion.

nettie – Slang term for someone who likes to spend a lot of time on the internet.

newbie – Popular term for a new member of a newsgroup or mailing list.

newsgroup – A Usenet discussion group. Each newsgroup is a collection of messages, usually unedited and not checked by anyone ('unmoderated'). Messages can be placed within the newsgroup by anyone including you. It is rather like reading and sending public emails. The ever-growing newsgroups have been around for much longer than the world wide web, and are an endless source of information, gossip, news, entertainment, sex, politics, resources and ideas. The 80,000-plus newsgroups are collectively referred to as Usenet, and millions of people use it every day.

newsreader – A type of software that enables you to search, read, post and manage messages in a newsgroup. It will normally be supplied by your internet service provider when you first sign up, or preloaded on your new computer. The best known are Microsoft Outlook, and Netscape Messenger.

news server – A remote computer (e.g. your internet service provider) that enables you to access newsgroups. If you cannot get some or any newsgroups from your existing news server, use your favourite search engine to search for 'open news servers' – there are lots of them freely available. When you have found one you like, add it to your news reader by clicking on its name. The first time you do this, it may take 10 to 20 minutes to load the names of all the newsgroups onto your computer, but after that they open up in seconds whenever you want them.

nick – Nickname, an alias you can give yourself and use when entering a chat channel, rather than using your real name.

Nominet – The official body for registering domain names in the UK (for example web sites whose name ends in .co.uk).

Notepad – The most basic type of word processor that comes with a Windows PC. To find it, click Start, Programs, then Accessories. Its more powerful cousin is Wordpad.

online – The time you spend linked via a modem to the internet. You can keep your phone bill down by reducing online time. The opposite term is offline.

open source software – A type of freely modifiable software, such as Linux. A definition and more information can be found at: http://www.opensource.org

OS – The operating system in a computer, for example MS DOS (Microsoft Disk Operating System) or Windows 95/98/2000.

packet – The term for any small piece of data sent or received over the internet on your behalf by your internet service provider, and containing your address and the recipient's address. One email message for example may be transmitted as several different packets of information, reassembled at the other end to recre-

Glossary of internet terms

ate the message.

parking – Placing your web domain into storage until you want to use it at a later date

password – A word or series of letters and numbers that enables a user to access a file, computer or program. A passphrase is a password made by using more than one word.

patch – A small piece of software used to patch up a hole or defect ('bug') in a software program.

PC – Personal computer, based on IBM technology. It is distinct from the Apple Macintosh which uses a different operating system

PDA – Personal Digital Assistant a mobile phone, palm top or any other hand-held processor, typically used to access the internet.

pdf – Portable document format, a handy type of file produced using Adobe Acrobat software. It has universal applications for text and graphics.

Pentium – The name of a very popular microprocessor chip in personal computers, manufactured by Intel. The first Pentium IIIs were supplied with secret and unique personal identifiers, which ordinary people surfing the net were unwittingly sending out, enabling persons unknown to construct detailed user profiles. After a storm of protest, Pentium changed the technology so that this identifier could be disabled. If you buy or use a Pentium III computer you should be aware of this risk to your privacy when online.

PGP – Pretty Good Privacy. A proprietary method of encoding a message before transmitting it over the internet. With PGP, a message is first compressed then encoded with the help of keys. Just like the valuables in a locked safe, your message is safe unless a person has access to the right keys. Many governments (as in France today) would like complete access to people's private keys. New Labour wanted access to everyone's keys in the UK, but dropped the proposed legislation after widespread protests. Unlike in many countries, there is no general right to privacy in the UK.

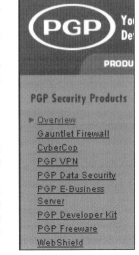

ping – You can use a ping test to check the connection speed between your computer and another computer.

plug-in – A type of (usually free and downloadable) software required to add some form of functionality to web page viewing. A well-known example is Macromedia Shockwave, a plug-in which enables you to view animations.

PoP – Point of presence. This refers to the dial-up phone numbers available from your ISP. If your ISP does not have a local point of presence (i.e. local access phone number), then don't sign up – your telephone bill will rocket because you will be charged national phone rates. All the major ISPs have local numbers covering the whole of the country.

portal site – Portal means gateway. It is a web site designed to be used as a 'home base' from which you can start your web experience each time you go online. Portals often serve as general information points and offer news, weather and other information that you can customise to your own needs. Yahoo! is a good example of a portal (http://www.yahoo.com). A portal site includes the one that loads into your browser each time you connect to the internet. It could for example be the front page of your internet service provider. Or you can set your browser to make it some other front page, for example a search engine such as Yahoo!, or even your own home page if you have one.

post, to – The common term used for sending ('posting') messages to a newsgroup. Posting messages is very like sending emails, except of course that they are public and everyone can read them. Also, newsgroup postings are archived, and can be read by anyone in the world years later. Because of this, many people feel more comfortable using an 'alias' (made-up name) when posting messages.

Glossary of internet terms ....

privacy – You have practically no personal privacy online. Almost every mouse click and key stroke you make while online is being electronically logged, analysed and possibly archived by internet organisations, government agencies, police or other surveillance services. You are also leaving a permanent trail of data on your computer. But then, if you have nothing to hide you have nothing to fear... To explore privacy issues worldwide visit the authoritative Electronic Frontier Foundation web site at http://www.eff.org, and for the UK, http://www.netfreedom.org.

protocol – Technical term for the method by which computers communicate. A protocol is something that has been agreed and can be used between systems. For example, for viewing web pages your computer would use hypertext transfer protocol (http). For downloading and uploading files, it would use file transfer protocol (ftp). It's not something to worry too much about in ordinary life.

proxy – An intermediate computer or server, used for reasons of security.

Quicktime – A popular free software program from Apple Computers. It is designed to play sounds and images including video clips and animations on both Apple Macs and personal computers.

radio button – A button which, when clicked, looks like this: ⊙

refresh, reload – The refresh or reload button on your browser toolbar tells the web page you are looking at to reload.

register – You may have to give your name, personal details and financial information to some sites before you can continue to use the pages. Site owners may want to produce a mailing list to offer you products and services. Registration is also used to discourage casual traffic.

registered user – Someone who has filled out an online form and then been granted permission to access a restricted area of a web site. Access is usually obtained by logging on, typically by entering a password and user name.

remailer – A remailer preserves your privacy by acting as a go-between when you browse or send email messages. An anonymous remailer is simply a computer connected to the internet that can forward an email message to other people after stripping off the header of the messages. Once a message is routed through an anonymous remailer, the recipient of that message, or anyone intercepting it, can no longer identify its origin.

RFC – Request for comment. RFCs are the way that the internet developers propose changes and discuss standards and procedures. See http://rs.internic.net.

RSA – One of the most popular methods of encryption, and used in Netscape browsers. See http://www.rsa.com.

router – A machine that direct internet data (network packets) from one internet location to another.

rules – The term for message filters in Outlook Express.

search engine – A search engine is a web site you can use for finding something on the internet. The technology variously involves the use of 'bots' (search robots), spiders or crawlers. Popular search engines have developed into big web sites and information centres in their own right. There are hundreds of them. Among the best known are AltaVista, Excite, Infoseek, Lycos, Metasearch and Webcrawler. See also **internet directories**.

secure servers – The hardware and software provided so that people can use their credit cards and leave other details without the risk of others seeing them online. Your browser will tell you when you are entering a secure site.

secure sockets layer (SSL) – A standard piece of technology which ensures secure financial transactions and data flow over the internet.

security certificate – Information that is used by the SSL protocol to establish a secure connection. Security certificates contain information about who it

Glossary of internet terms

belongs to, who it was issued by, some form of unique identification, valid dates, and an encrypted fingerprint that can be used to verify the contents of the certificate. In order for an SSL connection to be created both sides must have a valid security certificate.

server – Any computer on a network that provides access and serves information to other computers.

shareware – Software that you can try before you buy. Usually there is some kind of limitation such as an expiry date. To get the registered version, you must pay for the software, typically $20 to $40. A vast amount of shareware is now available on the internet.

Shockwave – A popular piece of software produced by Macromedia, which enables you to view animations and other special effects on web sites. You can download it free and in a few minutes from Macromedia's web site. The effects can be fun, but they slow down the speed at which the pages load into your browser window.

signature file – This is a little text file in which you can place your address details, for adding to email and newsgroup messages. Once you have created a signature file, it is appended automatically to your emails. You can of course delete or edit it.

Slashdot – One of the leading technology news web sites, found at: http://slashdot.org

smiley – A form of **emoticon**.

snail mail – The popular term for the standard postal service involving post-persons, vans, trains, planes, sacks and sorting offices.

sniffer – A program on a computer system (usually an ISP's system) designed to collect information. Sniffers are often used by hackers to harvest passwords and user names.

spam – The popular term for electronic junk mail – unsolicited and unwelcome email messages sent across the internet. There are various forms of spam-busting software which you can now obtain to filter out unwanted email messages.

SSL – Secure socket layer, a key part of internet security technology.

subscribe – The term for accessing a newsgroup in order to read and post messages in the newsgroup. There is no charge, and you can subscribe, unsubscribe and resubscribe at will with a click of your mouse. Unless you post a message, no one in the newsgroup will know that you have subscribed or unsubscribed.

surfing – Slang term for browsing the internet, especially following trails of links on pages across the world wide web.

sysop – Systems operator, someone rather like a moderator for example of a chat room or bulletin board service.

talkers – Servers which give users the opportunity to talk to each other. You connect to them, take a 'nickname' and start chatting. Usually, they offer some other features besides just allowing users to talk to each other, including Bulletin Boards, a 'world' such as a city or building, which you move around in. an opportunity to store some information on yourself, and some games.

TCP/IP – Transmission control protocol/internet protocol, the essential technology of the internet. It's not normally something to worry about.

telnet – Software that allows you to connect via the internet to a remote computer and work as if you were a terminal linked to that system.

theme – A term in web page design. A theme describes the general colours and graphics used within a web site. Many themes are available in the form of readymade templates.

thread – An ongoing topic in a Usenet newsgroup or mailing list discussion. The term refers to the original message on a particular topic, and all the replies and

Glossary of internet terms

other messages which spin off from it. With news reading software, you can easily 'view thread' and thus read the related messages in a convenient batch.

thumbnail – A small version of a graphic file which, when clicked, expands to a larger size.

top level domain – The last code in the domain name, such as .com or .uk

traceroute – A program that traces the route from your machine to a remote system. It is useful if you need to discover a person's ISP, for example in the case of a spammer.

traffic – The amount of data flowing across the internet, to a particular web site, newsgroup or chat room, or as emails.

trojan horse – A program that seems to perform a useful task but is really a malevolent program designed to cause damage to a computer system.

UNIX – This is a computer operating system that has been in use for many years, and still is used in many larger systems. Most ISPs use it.

uploading – The act of copying files from your PC to a server or other PC on the internet, for example when you are publishing your own web pages. The term is most commonly used to describe the act of copying HTML pages onto the internet via FTP.

URL – Uniform resource locator, the address of each internet page. For instance the URL of Internet Handbooks is http://www.internet-handbooks.co.uk

Usenet – The collection of well over 80,000 active newsgroups that make up a substantial part of the internet.

virtual reality – The presentation of a lifelike scenario in electronic form. It can be used for gaming, business or educational purposes.

virtual server – A portion of a PC that is used to host your own web domain (if you have one).

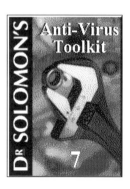

virus – A computer program maliciously designed to cause havoc to people's computer files. Viruses can typically be received when downloading program files from the internet, or from copying material from infected disks. Even Word files can now be infected. You can protect yourself from the vast majority of them by installing some inexpensive anti-virus software, such as Norton, McAfee or Dr Solomon.

WAP – Wireless Application Protocol, new technology that enables mobile phones to access the internet.

web – Short for the world wide web. See **WWW** below.

web authoring – Creating HTML pages to upload onto the internet. You will be a web author if you create your own home page for uploading onto the internet.

web-based chat – A form of internet chat which is conducted just using web pages, and not requiring special software like IRC and ICQ. For web-based chat, your browser must be Java-enabled. Most modern browsers are Java-enabled by default.

web client – Another term for a browser.

Webcrawler – A popular internet search engine used to find pages relating to specific keywords entered.

webmaster – Any person who manages a web site.

web page – Any single page of information you can view on the world wide web. A typical web page includes a unique URL (address), headings, text, images, and hyperlinks (usually in the form of graphic icons, or underlined text). One web page usually contains links to lots of other web pages, either within the same web site or elsewhere on the world wide web.

web rings – A network of interlinked web sites that share a common interest.

web site – A set of web pages, owned or managed by the same person or organisation, and which are interconnected by hyperlinks.

Whois – A network service that allows you to consult a database containing information about someone. A whois query can, for example, help to find the

Glossary of internet terms

identity of someone who is sending you unwanted email messages.

Windows – The ubiquitous operating system for personal computers developed by Bill Gates and the Microsoft Corporation. The Windows 3.1 version was followed by Windows 95, further enhanced by Windows 98. Windows 2000 is the latest.

WWW – The world wide web. Since it began in 1994 this has become the most popular part of the internet. The web is now made up of more than a billion web pages of every imaginable description, typically linking to other pages. Developed by the British computer scientist, Tim Berners-Lee, its growth has been exponential and looks set to continue so.

WYSIWYG – 'What you see is what you get.' If you see it on the screen, then it should look just the same when you print it out.

Yahoo! – Probably the world's most popular internet directory and search engine, and now valued on Wall Street at billions of dollars: http://www.yahoo.com

zip/unzip – Many files that you download from the internet will be in compressed format, especially if they are large files. This is to make them quicker to download. These files are said to be zipped or compressed. Unzipping these compressed files means returning them to their original size on receipt. Zip files have the extension '.zip' and are created (and unzipped) using WinZip or a similar popular software package.

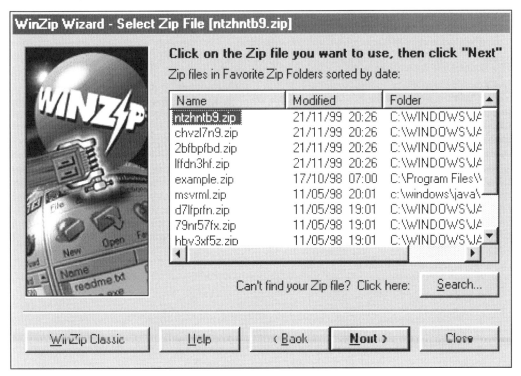

Visit the free Internet HelpZone at
www.internet-handbooks.co.uk
Helping you master the internet

Index

Active server pages, 30
Adobe GoLive, 22
advertising, 83, 85, 92, 93
Advertising Standards Authority, 93
affiliate programmes, 89
Aleph search, 53
Allsearch engines, 54
AltaVista, 39
Amazon.com, 12, 13, 96
analysing meta tags, 26
Ask Jeeves, 41
automated meta tags, 24
awards, 61

banner exchanges, 75
banner links, 63
Banner Warehouse, 63
bCentral, 36, 37, 57, 73, 76, 83, 90
Be Free, 89
branding, 11, 13
Bullet Mail, 86
Business Wire, 87

Chartered Institute of Marketing, 95
click through, 75, 82
Clipart UK, 14
Commission Junction, 89
Compaq, 39
cookies, 44
Copywriter, 87
crawlers, 31, 52
Cyber Eye, 24

databases, 30, 89, 94
data protection, 71
design, 17
Design Directory, 15
direct mail, 94
Direct Marketing Association, 94
directories, 52
Disney, 44
domain names, 16
DoubleClick, 84
dynamic pages, 30

Eboz, 75
Ecommerce Research Room, 89
Electronic Direct Marketing, 86
email, 70
email advertising, 85
email newsletters, 74
Excite, 42, 47, 82
exhibitions, 96
Exploit Submission Wizard, 33

Ezine Factory, 74
ezines, 74, 85

frames, 28, 29
Free for all links, 64
FrontPage, 22, 24, 25

Galaxy, 81
Go.com, 44
GoTo, 81
Google, 43

Hi Verify, 26
Hollis Directories, 93
HotBot, 43, 58
HTML, 21

Idea Marketers, 78, 79
indexing, 29
industries, 54
InfoSeek, 44
Institute of Practitioners in Advertising, 93
Institute of Public Relations, 94
Institute of Sales Promotion, 96
International Public Relations Association, 94
Internet News Bureau, 87
Intersaver, 18

javascript, 30
journalists, 67
junk mail, 72

key words, 67

Leads Link, 86
Lifestyle Publishing, 85
LinkExchange, 76
Link Share, 90
links, 64, 66
List Bot, 73
location, 12
logos, 13, 92
LookSmart, 45, 82
Lycos, 43–45, 58

Macromedia Dreamweaver, 22
mailing lists, 73
Making Profit, 78
Market Research Society, 96
Media First, 68
MetaTag Maker, 25
meta tags, 21

117

Index

Metabot, 25
Met-tags.com, 24
Microsoft B Central, 28, 57, 76, 83
Microsoft FrontPage, 22, 24, 25
MSN, 45, 47

NetMechanic, 28
Netscape, 58, 65
newsgroups, 64
newsletters, 34, 74

offline promotion, 92
Open Directory Project, 58
Opt-in lists, 73, 86

page design, 30
Page Submit Pro, 33, 343
pay by impression, 81
paying for promotion, 80
Pop Up Exchange, 84
pop-ups, 84
PostMaster Direct, 86
PR Newswire, 88
PR Web, 70
press release distribution, 69
Press Release Network, 88
press release writing, 68
press releases, 67
Pro Boost, 28
promotion 18
public relations, 94

reciprocal links, 63, 64, 75
referrals, 89
repeat submissions, 37
robots, 31

scanning, 30
Scoot, 57
Scrub The Web, 48
search engine acceptability, 30
Search Engine Colossus, 55
Search Engine Watch, 26, 40
search engines, 20

searchability, 56
site promoting, 14
Snap, 48, 49
spamming, 72
spiders, 31, 41, 52
straplines, 92
Submit Corner, 24, 27
Submit It, 36, 57
Submit Wolf Pro, 34
submitting to search engines, 31

targeted email, 70, 86
text, 16
The Web Wire, 70
The Web Writer, 16, 23
title tag, 22
trade shows, 96
Traffic Builder, 35, 56, 64

UK Banners, 76
UK Plus, 47, 59
unsolicited email, 72
URL Wire, 90
Usenet, 64

Web Crawler, 49, 50
Web Position Gold, 26, 56
web reference, 14
web rings, 61
Web Wire, 70
Web Writer, 16, 23
Webs Unlimited, 25
What's New, 59
What's Nu, 60
Willings Press Guide, 93
Wilson Web, 77
word of mouth, 96
World Wide Mart, 64

Yahoo!, 34, 43, 45, 48, 50, 51, 54, 96
Yahoo! Business Express, 82
Yale Style Guide, 17
Yellow Pages, 59

Other Internet Handbooks

Books & Publishing on the Internet
An essential guide for authors, readers, editors, booksellers, librarians & publishing professionals
Roger Ferneyhough MA (Oxon)

Are you an author, bookseller, publisher or editor? Here is a guide to today's whole new world of books and publishing information online. The book reviews web sites of every imaginable kind – of publishers, bookstores, writers' groups, literary agents, book fairs, book distributors, training organisations, prizes, book-related associations, pressure groups, periodicals and many more. Whether you are planning to write, edit, publish or distribute a book, or want to contact a specialist, this is the book for you.
1 84025 332 0

Building a Web Site on the Internet
A practical guide to writing and commissioning web pages
Brendan Murphy BSc (Hons)

This book meets the urgent need for all business users who need an effective internet presence. Written in plain English, it explains the three main ways of achieving this: create it yourself by writing HTML, create it yourself by using a popular software package, or create it by hiring a web development company. Whether your organisation is large or small, make sure *you* make the right choices for your web site. Brendan Murphy BSc MBA MBSC teaches HNC in Computing, and lectures on the internet for the Open University. He is a Member of the British Computer Society, and Institute of Management Information Systems.
1 84025 314 2

Careers Guidance on the Internet
An essential guide to careers and vocational guidance resources online
Laurel Alexander

Are you planning to apply for a new job, or seeking promotion, or looking for new skills? Perhaps you are responsible for providing careers guidance to adults or young people? Careers information – like so many other things – is being challenged and revolutionised by the internet. New internet knowledge and skills are urgently needed by every professional working in this vital field. Packed with expert advice, and concise reviews of key web sites, this timely book will help you take full advantage of some amazing new online resources. Laurel Alexander MIPD MICG is a qualified trainer, assessor and guidance specialist.
1 84025 351 7

Chat & Chat Rooms on the Internet
A practical guide to exploring the live net chat communities
Mark Ray MSc

Whether you are a recent entrant into the internet world, an experienced web user, or even a dedicated operator of an Internet Relay Chat channel, this book provides an in-depth guide to talkers and IRC. It includes detailed snapshots of real online conversations, information on the major networks, and explains how to download and use the tested client software. Written with the help of some of those who make up these new communities, it also looks at how some have organised themselves into virtual democracies, how they are developing, and discusses where all this fantastic new technology may lead. Mark Ray MSc is the webmaster and system operator for the Union of University of East Anglia Students.
1 84025 347 9

Other Internet Handbooks

Creating a Home Page on the Internet
An illustrated step-by-step guide for beginners
Richard Cochrane BA(Hons) PhD

Have you just started to use the internet? If so you will soon be wondering how you can produce and publish web pages of your own, as millions of other individuals have done all over the world. It's easy! Discover how to design a simple but effective home page; see how to add your own artwork and photographs; learn how to add those magic hypertext links that enable you to click effortlessly from one web page to another. Finally, explore how you can actually publish your own home pages in cyberspace, where potentially anyone in the world can pay you a 'visit' and contact you by email.
1 84025 309 6

Discussion Forums on the Internet
A practical step-by-step guide to newsgroups, mailing lists and bulletin board services
Kye Valongo

A vast number of messages are posted into newsgroups, mailing lists and bulletin board services every day, and millions of people all over the world love to read them. These forums cover every imaginable subject, from local interest to jobs and travel, education, finance, entertainment, raunchy sex and scandal, culture and politics, computing and more. But how do you access them? Are they censored? How do you read the messages, and post messages yourself? Written in plain English, this guide tells you everything you need to know to explore this lively and ever controversial side of the internet. Kye Valongo is a qualified teacher, computer analyst, internet journalist and former Education Officer for IBM.
1 84025 329 0

Education & Training on the Internet
An essential resource for students, teachers, and education providers
Laurel Alexander MIPD MICG

Confused by search engines? Fed up with floods of irrelevant information? This is a much-needed new guide to today's exploding new world of education and training online. It includes reviews of top web sites of every imaginable kind – for education and training providers, schools, colleges, universities, training centres, professional organisations, resource suppliers, individuals, business organisations and academic institutions. Whether you are planning to study on-line, or are planning the delivery of online education and training, you will find this a key resource. Laurel Alexander MIPD MICG is a qualified trainer, assessor and guidance specialist.
1 84025 346 0

Finding a Job on the Internet
Amazing new possibilities for jobseekers everywhere
Brendan Murphy BSc (Hons) MBA MBSC

Thinking of looking for a new job, or even a change of career? The internet is a great place to start your job search. In easy steps and plain English, this new guide explains how to find and use internet web sites and newsgroups to give you what you need. School, college and university leavers will find it invaluable for identifying suitable employers and getting expert help with CVs and job applications. The book will also be useful for career advisers and employers thinking of using the internet for recruitment purposes. Brendan Murphy BSc MBA MBSC teaches HNC in Computing, and lectures for the Open University.
1 84025 310 X – reprinted

Other Internet Handbooks

Gardens & Gardening on the Internet
A practical handbook and reference guide to horticulture online
Judith & Graham Lawlor MA

Gardeners are often in need of specific information to help them in their projects, and the internet is proving an amazingly valuable new aid to modern gardening. This new book leads you quickly and painlessly to some amazing new gardening help lines, retail and wholesale suppliers, online clubs and societies, and web sites devoted to such topics as rare plants, water gardens, celebrity gardening, gardening holidays, and horticultural science. The book will be absolutely indispensable for all gardeners with access to the internet.
1 84025 313 4

Getting Connected to the Internet
A practical step-by-step guide for everyone
Ian Hosker

This book is intended for every PC owner who has not yet connected to the internet, but wants to do so provided they can feel confident about the process. It addresses all the questions commonly asked by the first-time subscriber. For example, what's the benefit of being online? What is an internet service provider (ISP)? What equipment do I need? What do I have to do, step-by-step? How do I send my first email? The book guides you carefully through all the initial stages. It shows how to get your computer ready, and how to load the required software from a CD. It explains how to create multiple email accounts, and perhaps most important of all, what to do if things don't go quite according to plan. Ian Hosker BEd(Hons) MSc is CVET Coordinator at the College of SS Mark & John in Plymouth.
1 84025 374 6

Getting Started on the Internet
A practical step-by-step guide for beginners
Kye Valongo

In plain English, this steps you through all the basics of the internet. It shows you how to obtain free access to the internet, how to set up your computer, how to look for information, and how to send and receive emails. It explains how to explore newsgroups and internet chat, how to protect your privacy online, and even how to create your own home page. Whether you want the internet for use at home, in education or in the workplace, this is the book for you, specially designed to get you up and running with the minimum fuss and bother. Kye Valongo is a qualified teacher, computer analyst, internet journalist and former Education Officer for IBM.
1 84025 321 5

Homes & Property on the Internet
A guide to 1000s of top web sites for buyers, sellers, owners, tenants, sharers, holiday makers & property professionals
Philip Harrison

Here is a guide to today's whole new world of homes and property services online. Here are web sites of every imaginable kind for estate agents, house builders, removal firms, decorators, town planners, architects and surveyors, banks and building societies, home shares, villa owners and renters, and property-related associations, pressure groups, newspapers and magazines. Whether you are planning to move house, or rent a holiday home, or locate property services in the UK or wider afield, this is the book for you – comprehensive and well-indexed to help you find what you want.
1 84025 335 5

Other Internet Handbooks................................

Internet Explorer on the Internet
A step-by-step guide to using your browser
Kye Valongo

This book tells you all about Internet Explorer, the world's most popular and powerful browser. In practical steps, it explains how to use it for surfing the internet, how to send and read email messages using Outlook, and how to manage your electronic Address Book. Learn how to store selected web pages as Favourites (bookmarks). Discover how to disable irritating cookies. Find out how to control or delete sensitive computer files. If you are using Internet Explorer, or sharing access to a computer, this book will boost both your pleasure and protection when using the internet. Kye Valongo is a qualified teacher, computer analyst, internet journalist and former Education Officer for IBM.
1 84025 334 7

The Internet for Schools
A practical step-by-step guide for teachers, student teachers, parents and governors
Barry Thomas & Richard Williams

This title is aimed at teachers, student teachers, parents and school governors – in fact anyone interested in using the internet in primary and secondary education. The format is entertaining with key points highlighted. Each chapter is free-standing and should take no more than fifteen minutes to read. A major aim is to explain things in clear, non-technical and non-threatening language. There are detailed reviews of many key educational internet sites. Written by two experienced IT teachers, the book is UK focused, and contains typical examples and practical tasks that could be undertaken with students.
1 84025 302 9

The Internet for Students
Making the most of the new medium for study and fun
David Holland ACIB

Are you a student needing help with the internet to pursue your studies? Not sure where to start? – then this Internet Handbook is the one for you. It's up to date, full of useful ideas of places to visit on the internet, written in a clear and readable style, with plenty of illustrations and the minimum of jargon. It is the ideal introduction for all students who want to add interest to their studies, and make their finished work stand out, impressing lecturers and future employers alike. The internet is going to bring about enormous changes in modern life. As a student, make sure you are up to speed.
1 84025 306 1 – Reprinted

The Internet for Writers
Using the new medium to research, promote and publish your work
Nick Daws BSc (Hons)

This guide offers all writers with a complete introduction to the internet – how to master the basic skills, and how to use this amazing new medium to create, publish and promote your creative work. Would you like to broaden and speed up your research? Meet fellow writers, editors and publishers through web sites, newsgroups, or chat? Even publish your work on the internet for a potentially enormous new audience? Then this is the book you need, with all the practical starting points to get you going, step by step. The book is a selection of *The UK Good Book Guide*.
1 84025 308 8

Other Internet Handbooks

Internet Skills for the Workplace
Empowering yourself for the digital age
Ian Hosker

The internet is fast becoming an essential tool in the workplace. This book is intended for everyone employed, or hoping to become employed, for any organisation that makes use of the internet in its daily activities. It helps you learn how to send, manage and reply to emails in a business setting, how to use a web browser, and how to research information using the internet. With its structured approach to learning specific new skills, the book makes an ideal companion for people taking City & Guilds and other training courses in internet competence. Ian Hosker BEd(Hons) MSc is CVET Coordinator at the College of SS Mark & John in Plymouth.
1 84025 328 2

Law & Lawyers on the Internet
An essential guide and resource for legal practitioners
Stephen Hardy JP LLB PhD

Following the Woolf Reforms, efficient research and communication will be the key to future legal life. This handbook will meet the needs of solicitors, barristers, law students, public officials, community groups and consumers who are seeking guidance on how to access and use the major legal web sites and information systems available to them on the internet. It includes expert site reviews on law associations, law firms, case law and court reporting, European legal institutions, government, legal education and training, publishers, the courts and branches of the law. Don't leave for court without it! Stephen Hardy JP LLB PhD teaches law at the University of Manchester Business School.
1 84025 345 2

Marketing Your Business on the Internet (2nd edition)
A practical step-by-step guide for all business owners and managers
Sara Edlington

Written by someone experienced in marketing on the internet from its earliest days, this practical book will show you step-by-step how to make a success of marketing your organisation on the internet. Discover how to find a profitable on-line niche, know which ten essential items to have on your web site, how to keep visitors returning again and again, how to secure valuable on- and off-line publicity for your organisation, and how to build your brand online. The internet is set to create phenomenal new marketing opportunities – make sure you are ready to win your share.
1 84025 364 9 (2nd edition)

Medicine & Health on the Internet
A practical guide to online advice, treatments, doctors and support groups
Sarah Wilkinson

In the last couple of years, thousands of new health and medical web sites have been launched on the internet. Do you want to find out about a specialist treatment or therapy? Do you want to contact a support group or clinician online, or perhaps just get the answer to a simple question? Don't get lost using search engines. Whether you are a patient, relative, carer, doctor, health administrator, medical student or nurse, this book will lead you quickly to all the established web sites you need – help lines, support groups, hospitals, clinics and hospices, health insurance and pharmaceutical companies, treatments, suppliers, professional bodies, journals, and more.
1 84025 337 1

Other Internet Handbooks

Naming a Web Site on the Internet
How to choose, register and protect the right domain name for your web site
Graham Jones BSc(Hons)

Would you like to obtain a proper domain name for your own web site, for example 'dot.com' or 'dot.co.uk'? Perhaps you have a name in mind, but are not sure how to register it. Do you know the rules which govern the naming of web sites? This valuable handbook explains just how to choose and register your own 'domain name' on the world wide web. The official rules are clearly explained, with lots of practical examples to help you. There are many places you can apply for a domain name and a bewildering array of prices and conditions. This book provides a clear step-by-step guide through the maze. It also explains how to protect your domain names, where to 'host' them, and how to move them from one machine to another. The rush is on – act now to register and protect the names you want.
1 84025 359 2

Personal Finance on the Internet
Your complete online guide to savings, investment, loans, mortgages, pensions, insurance and all aspects of personal finance
Graham Jones BSc(Hons)

For many people the internet is now the preferred means of managing their personal finances. But how do you do it? Where can you check out financial products and services on the internet? How secure is it, and what are the risks? Step-by-step this book explains what you need to run your finances on the internet, where to find financial information, managing your bank account online, getting credit via the internet, checking out mortgages, saving your money online, buying and selling stocks and shares online, arranging your pensions and insurance online, paying taxes, and much more. Graham Jones BSc(Hons) is an Associate Lecturer with the Open University and author of 17 books on internet and business topics.
1 84025 320 7

Shops & Shopping on the Internet
A practical guide to online stores, catalogues, retailers and shopping malls
Kathy Lambert

In the last couple of years, thousands of shops and stores have been launched on the internet. But what are they like? Where can you find your favourite brands and stores? What about deliveries from suppliers in the UK or overseas? Can you safely pay by credit card? Don't get stuck in the internet traffic! This carefully structured book will take you quickly to all the specialist stores, virtual shopping malls, and online catalogues of your choice. You will be able to compare prices, and shop till you drop for books, magazines, music, videos, clothes, holidays, electrical goods, games and toys, wines, and a vast array of other goods and services.
1 84025 327 4

Studying English on the Internet
An A to Z guide to useful electronic resources freely available on the internet
Wendy Shaw BSc(Hons)

Written by a university researcher, this new guide has been specially collated for the internet user of all levels in the discipline of English. Whether you are a student, teacher, tutor or lecturer, this is the guide for you. It offers a clear and graphical presentation of web sites and electronic resources on the internet for both teaching and research purposes. The A-Z format makes it easy to pick out an author or electronic text centre from the bulleted list. Hundreds of key gateway web sites for English Studies are reviewed in this valuable course companion.
1 84025 317 7

Other Internet Handbooks

Studying Law on the Interent
How to use the internet for learning and study, exams and career development
Stephen Hardy JP LLB PhD

Are you studying law at college or university, or as a distance learner? Do you have internet access? Computers and the internet are becoming ever more important in both legal learning and practice today. The internet in particular is a rich legal resource for barristers, solicitors, legal executives and officials alike. This handbook meets the needs of law students wanting quick access to the major relevant legal web sites and legal information systems available over the internet. Use this book to expand your knowledge, develop your skills, and greatly improve your career prospects. Stephen Hardy JP LLB PhD teaches law at the University of Manchester Business School.
1 84025 370 3

Travel & Holidays on the Internet
The amazing new world of online travel services, information, prices, reservations, timetables, bookings and more
Graham Jones BSc(Hons)

Thinking of checking out flights to Europe or America, or booking a package holiday? The internet is the best place to start. In easy steps and plain English, this book explains how to find and use the web to locate the travel and holiday information you need. You can view the insides of hotels, villas and even aeroplanes, quickly compare costs and services, and make your reservations and bookings securely online. You'll be amazed at how much more you'll find with the help of this remarkable book. Graham Jones BSc(Hons) is an Associate Lecturer with the Open University and author of 17 books on internet and business topics.
1 84025 325 8

Using Credit Cards on the Internet
A practical step-by-step guide for all cardholders and retailers
Graham Jones BSc(Hons)

Are you worried about using credit cards on the internet? This valuable book shows you how to avoid trouble and use your 'virtual plastic' in complete safety over the internet. It contains all the low-down on security, practical tips to make sure that all your credit card dealings are secure, and advice on where to find credit cards with extra 'web protection'. If you are running a business on the internet, it also explains how to set up a 'merchant account' so that customers can safely pay you using their credit cards. The book is complete with a guide to the best web sites on credit card usage. Graham Jones BSc(Hons) is an Associate Lecturer with the Open University and author of 17 books on internet and business topics.
1 84025 349 5

Using Email on the Internet
A step-by-step guide to sending and receiving messages and files
Kye Valongo

Email is one of the oldest parts of the internet. Most newcomers approach it with a bit of trepidation. But don't worry – it is quite straightforward and easy. Emailing is fast, cheap and convenient, and you'll soon wonder how you ever managed without it. Use this book to find out how to get started, how to successfully send and receive your first messages, how to send and receive attached files, how to manage your email folders, address book, user profiles, personal privacy, and lots more valuable skills. Kye Valongo is a qualified teacher, computer analyst, internet journalist and former Education Officer for IBM.
1 84025 300 2

Other Internet Handbooks

Where to Find It on the Internet (2nd edition)
Your complete guide to search engines, portals, databases, yellow pages & other internet reference tools
Kye Valongo

Here is a valuable basic reference guide to hundreds of carefully selected web sites for everyone wanting to track down information on the internet. Don't waste time with fruitless searches – get to the sites you want, fast. This book provides a complete selection of the best search engines, online databases, directories, libraries, people finders, yellow pages, portals, and other powerful research tools. A recent selection of *The Good Book Guide*, and now in a new edition, this book will be an essential companion for all internet users, whether at home, in education, or in the workplace. Kye Valongo is a qualified teacher, computer analyst, internet journalist and former Education Officer for IBM.
1 84025 369 X – 2nd edition

Wildlife & Conservation on the Internet
An essential guide to environmental resources online
Kate Grey BSc(Hons)

Are you interested in the future of our natural heritage? Perhaps you are a student or teacher of environmental studies, or with a job in this responsible area? Here is a unique guide to wildlife trusts, official and public organisations, coastal and marine web sites, nature reserves, zoos, national parks, and thousands more on-line resources. With its expert reviews, this timely book is essential reference for town and country dwellers, officials and planners, conservationists, and everyone interested in environmental issues. It is also a valuable resource for primary and secondary schools and teachers, and college lecturers, using the internet for educational purposes.
1 84025 318 5

Working from Home on the Internet
A practical illustrated guide for everyone
Laurel Alexander MIPD MICG

Would you like to work from home and earn good money using communications technology and the internet? More than 300 top sites are reviewed in this book which detail business opportunities on the internet, employers who use home workers and teleworkers, as well as recruitment agencies for IT and internet work. There are also sections on finding capital, legislation for the self employed, support for home workers (including disabled workers), business services and suppliers on the internet, and internet-based learning. Laurel Alexander MIPD MICG is a qualified trainer, assessor and guidance specialist.
1 84025 371 1

Your Privacy on the Internet
Everything you need to know about protecting your privacy and security online
Kye Valongo

Is Big Brother watching you? Many people will be shocked to hear that eavesdropping on private electronic communication is relatively easy and commonplace. This book explores the alarming way in which governments, companies and hackers are all using the internet to threaten your privacy. It also explains the various types of software you can use to prevent snooping and protect your privacy, whether you are browsing web pages, sending or receiving emails, accessing newsgroups, using search engines, or transmitting or receiving any kind of data online. The new borderless world is changing the whole way we live. Stay alert, and keep ahead. Kye Valongo is a qualified teacher, computer analyst, internet journalist and former Education Officer for IBM.
1 84025 355 X